The Diabetic
Pastry Chef

The *Diabetic* Pastry Chef

Stacey Harris

PELICAN PUBLISHING COMPANY
GRETNA 2010

*The word "Pelican" and the depiction of a pelican are trademarks
of Pelican Publishing Company, Inc., and are registered in the
U.S. Patent and Trademark Office.*

Library of Congress Cataloging-in-Publication Data

Harris, Stacey, 1951-
  The diabetic pastry chef / by Stacey Harris.
     p. cm.
  Includes index.
  ISBN 978-1-58980-747-1 (hardcover : alk. paper) 1. Diabetes—Diet
therapy—Recipes. 2. Pastry. I. Title.
  RC662.H377 2010
  641.5'6314–dc22

                                    2009025890

This book is meant to be a cookbook, not a medical manual. It is not
intended as a dietary prescription. All persons with health concerns
should seek the advice of a qualified medical professional such as a
physician, registered diabetes educator, or registered dietician. The Food
and Drug Administration has determined sucralose to be safe for everyone,
but consuming sucralose or Splenda® is done at your own risk. Neither
the author nor the publisher is affiliated with the manufacturer, McNeil
Specialty Products, and is not liable for the product.

Printed in the United States of America

Published by Pelican Publishing Company, Inc.
1000 Burmaster Street, Gretna, Louisiana 70053

This book is dedicated to my late beloved mother, Evelyn Dolores Harris; my grandmother Nellie Jackson; my great-aunt, Rebecca Gross; my aunts, Josephine Barber and Lillian Sloan; and my dear cousin, Marilyn Barber.
All were great cooks and bakers,
and all were diabetics.

Contents

Acknowledgments

Special thanks to my husband, Howard Marshall; my amazing daughter, Tara Michelle Catherine Harris; my supportive sisters Victoria Harris, Deborah Hall, and Gwen Cloutier; my dear friends Vern Coker and Annette Sersich; my nutritionist, Linda H. Brown; my recipe tester, Paddy Lanthier; my valuable agent, Rick Broadhead; and the incredible folks at Pelican Publishing Company, who helped to make all of this possible.

Abbreviations

tsp.	=	teaspoon
tbsp.	=	tablespoon
oz.	=	ounce
qt.	=	quart
lb.	=	pound

Standard-Metric Approximations

⅛ teaspoon		=		.6 milliliter
¼ teaspoon		=		1.2 milliliters
½ teaspoon		=		2.5 milliliters
1 teaspoon		=		5 milliliters
1 tablespoon		=		15 milliliters
4 tablespoons	=	¼ cup	=	60 milliliters
8 tablespoons	=	½ cup	=	118 milliliters
16 tablespoons	=	1 cup	=	236 milliliters
2 cups		=		473 milliliters
2 ½ cups		=		563 milliliters
4 cups		=		946 milliliters
1 quart	=	4 cups	=	.94 liter

Solid Measurements

½ ounce		=		15 grams
1 ounce		=		25 grams
4 ounces		=		110 grams
16 ounces	=	1 pound	=	454 grams

Introduction

I have been baking and collecting recipes and cookbooks since the age of 13, when I took my first home economics class in junior high school. My phenomenal mother, Evelyn Dolores Harris, a consummate baker, had not permitted me to bake in her well-appointed kitchen up until this time. She was pleased, however, to see me take such an interest in baking, as she was a proud housewife who tremendously enjoyed cooking, baking, cleaning, decorating, and caring for her family in general. She began to encourage my newfound interest in the culinary arts and discussed with me the techniques, formulas, and recipes I was bringing home from school. She finally opened up her coveted kitchen to me so I could commence cooking, baking, and experimenting on my own. I could tell that my mother was quite pleased to have me following in her padded-slipper footsteps.

One of the first novelty recipes I learned in home ec was Easter Basket Cupcakes, capped with white icing, green-tinted coconut, a sprinkling of colorful jellybeans, and white pipe cleaners for handles. To this day, every Easter, I still enjoy making this recipe.

As I became an adult, I cooked and baked my way through life while holding down a full-time job as a mortgage banker. I would often bake for my co-workers, which always made me the darling of the office.

When it looked as though the mortgage industry was about to take a downturn several years ago, I enrolled in culinary school with the intention of becoming a big, well-known pastry chef. Halfway through school, which consisted of a 12-month Le Cordon Bleu course, I became ill and was subsequently operated on for a serious stomach ailment. While in the hospital, I received the unwelcome news that I was diabetic. I would have to give up sweets, including baking them, which would undoubtedly be too tempting for me.

I was devastated. Baking was supposed to become my second

career, the one that would rescue me from the impending unemployment line. Next followed a brief period of depression as I tried to figure out another course of action. I had been collecting recipes and devising my own line of gourmet bakery items for years, even before I began attending culinary school. *What could I do with these recipes now?* What a waste of recipes, what a waste of a life, I thought. But after the "oh, woe is me" period, I began to pull myself together and entertain the thought of developing a line of diabetic-friendly pastries. I have to admit, though, that I wasn't too enthused about the prospect, as I had tasted low-carb and sugar-free products in the past that left a lot to be desired. These products were consistently bad. The bakers mistakenly thought their diabetic food products could not be improved upon. Still, I had no choice. I could not continue to eat as I had in the past if I wanted to maintain my health.

So I began to slowly experiment, at first with dismal results, confirming my initial fears that diabetic desserts were tasteless and disappointing. The low-carb fad was in full force at the time, so I began to read low-carb and other healthy cookbooks, picking up dietary tips along the way. I incorporated them into my recipes. I learned about the dangers of white flour, refined sugar, and trans fats and the havoc they were wreaking on our systems. So I began to blend my flours and reduce the sugar or combine it with artificial sweeteners. I totally eliminated trans fats (though I sorely missed my piecrusts), and I learned to cut milk carbs in half. Hallelujah! I realized I was on to something good. My desserts still tasted great after all of these changes. I was somehow able to retain the satisfying tastes of my original recipes. Even my family and friends had to agree, and not because I twisted their arms!

I began to share my tips, techniques, and recipes on a diabetes Internet forum. They were so well received that I called myself the Diabetic Pastry Chef and started a Web site. I was pleased to now have a renewed purpose in life, one that was more meaningful than my previous one. I am now in a position to help millions of suffering diabetics like myself still be able to enjoy delicious desserts while continuing to maintain their health.

Sugar is of course the standard sweetener for most desserts, white flour the standard flour, and butter the standard fat. These ingredients provide a certain taste, appearance, and texture we have all come to expect in our baked goods. When a different ingredient is substituted, the outcome is altered and generally deemed inferior. Diabetics are told to severely limit sugar, white flour, and fats—the basis for most baked goods. This does not leave us with the best of options, and it proves to be a major challenge in devising quality recipes. I took all of these factors into consideration when I began to develop diabetic-friendly dessert recipes. I feel that my formula, when experimented with, will produce the finest diabetic-friendly pastries possible. And these are recipes the whole family can enjoy!

Here's the Gist of What I Do

We are all dealing with our diets differently. Some diabetics like high-fat, low-carb diets. Others like low-fat, low-carb diets. Some follow the exchange diet or one of the many other diabetic diets. There are diabetics who won't touch Splenda®, others who avoid gluten, etc. I'm sure you get the point.

The recipes I share are my own personal recipes. These recipes work well for my health and glucose readings. My body may produce more or less insulin than yours. My cholesterol levels may differ from yours, as well as my taste buds. When you're dealing with diabetes, one recipe does not fit all. You have to be able to tailor a recipe to your specific health preferences and taste buds. You have to be able to take a recipe and make it your own.

I've provided a formula and many tips to help you accomplish this. I pray you never look at a recipe again and think, "I can't make that. It has too much sugar, too many carbs, or too much fat, or it contains white flour or wheat," etc. My formula should enable you to pick up any cookbook or go to any baking site and convert almost any dessert recipe to a diabetic-friendly version you are able to eat and enjoy without worry.

My formula consists of 4 parts: (1) change or mix the flours, (2) reduce the sugar, (3) dilute whole milk with half water, and (4) use a healthier fat such as canola oil. These 4 steps should be enough to adequately convert most of the dessert recipes you come across, but if not, I provide a host of additional tips that can be utilized to lower the carbs and/or fat even further. The results are pretty much the same as the traditional recipe—and sometimes even better! Trust me, you don't have to limit the desserts you can eat and enjoy, as long as you successfully make the recipe your own.

I make my own low-carb flours, which I use to prepare pancakes, waffles, and muffins. I keep the following on hand at all times: white flour, white whole-wheat flour, whole-wheat flour, soy flour, whole almonds, and old-fashioned oats. I am continually adding new flours to my arsenal.

If I'm making muffins, I follow a traditional recipe that, for example, calls for 3 cups flour. I look at my flours and might decide to mix 1 cup white flour, 1 cup whole-wheat flour, and 1 cup soy flour together. Occasionally, I use all whole-wheat flour or any other mixture I prefer. I sometimes grind almonds to make almond flour or oats to make oat flour.

I am not a big fan of baking with artificial sweeteners, as they alter the texture and flavors too much and make things stick to the pan. When baking cakes or muffins, I prefer to *reduce* the amount of sugar rather than use all artificial sweetener or even a combination of sweetener and sugar. For instance, I recently baked a large batch of Amish Raisin Bran Muffins that called for 3 cups sugar. I reduced the sugar to 1 cup with very satisfactory results.

I've discovered that a combination of half sugar and half Splenda® works well in sweet potato and pumpkin pies, baked breads, rice puddings (I use brown rice), and custards. I also use half sugar and half Splenda® when I bake pies such as apple, pineapple, peach, or berry. These pies taste pretty much the same as if I had used all sugar.

If a recipe calls for oil, I use canola oil. If a recipe calls for butter, I will generally use canola butter or Smart Balance® regular spread.

I purchase whole milk, and when cooking, I mix it with half water to make an approximate 2 percent milk. This cuts the carbs (as well as the price of the milk!) in half. There is no noticeable difference in taste from 2 percent milk.

These recipes are not the final word. They are here to get you to experiment with the dessert recipes you come across until you obtain a level of control that is comfortable to you, your health, and your taste buds. This can be achieved by monitoring portions, reducing the recipe ingredients that adversely affect your health, and adding or substituting those that help. Use your own discretion, and seek the advice of your licensed healthcare provider.

Carb and other nutritional counts are included with these recipes. When a choice of ingredients is offered, the first listed was used in the nutritional counts. Please note that the percentages that make up the calorie counts will vary between 99 and 101, due to rounding individual values up or down. Should you choose to substitute different ingredients, a carb counter is also included at the end of the book.

Diabetic Pastry Chef

The Diabetic
Pastry Chef

Chapter 1

Diabetes

What Is Diabetes?

Diabetes is a group of diseases marked by high levels of blood glucose, also called blood sugar, resulting from defects in insulin production, insulin action, or both. Diabetes can lead to serious complications and premature death, but people with diabetes can take steps to control the disease and lower the risk of complications.

Types of Diabetes

Type 1 diabetes was previously called insulin-dependent diabetes mellitus (IDDM) or juvenile-onset diabetes. Type 1 diabetes develops when the body's immune system destroys pancreatic beta cells, the only cells in the body that make the hormone insulin that regulates blood glucose. To survive, people with type 1 diabetes must have insulin delivered by injection or a pump. This form of diabetes usually strikes children and young adults, although disease onset can occur at any age. In adults, type 1 diabetes accounts for 5 to 10 percent of all diagnosed cases of diabetes. Risk factors for type 1 diabetes may be autoimmune, genetic, or environmental. No known way to prevent type 1 diabetes exists. Several clinical trials for the prevention of type 1 diabetes are currently in progress or are being planned.

Type 2 diabetes was previously called non-insulin-dependent diabetes mellitus (NIDDM) or adult-onset diabetes. In adults, type 2 diabetes accounts for about 90 to 95 percent of all diagnosed cases of diabetes. It usually begins as insulin resistance, a disorder in which the cells do not use insulin properly. As the need for insulin rises, the pancreas gradually loses its ability to produce it. Type 2 diabetes is associated with older age, obesity, family history of diabetes, history of gestational diabetes, impaired glucose metabolism, physical inactivity, and race/ethnicity. African-Americans, Hispanic/Latino Americans, American Indians, and some Asian Americans and Native Hawaiians or other Pacific Islanders are at particularly high risk for type 2 diabetes and its complications. Type 2 diabetes in children and adolescents, although still rare, is being diagnosed more frequently among American Indians, African-Americans, Hispanic/Latino Americans, and Asians/Pacific Islanders.

Gestational diabetes is a form of glucose intolerance diagnosed during pregnancy. Gestational diabetes occurs more frequently among African-Americans, Hispanic/Latino Americans, and American Indians. It is also more common among obese women and women with a family history of diabetes. During pregnancy, gestational diabetes requires treatment to normalize maternal blood glucose levels to avoid complications in the infant. Immediately after pregnancy, 5 to 10 percent of women with gestational diabetes are found to have diabetes, usually type 2. Women who have had gestational diabetes have a 40 to 60 percent chance of developing diabetes in the next 5 to 10 years.

Other types of diabetes result from specific genetic conditions, surgery, medications, infections, pancreatic disease, and other illnesses. Such types of diabetes account for 1 to 5 percent of all diagnosed cases.

Treating Diabetes

Diabetes can lead to serious complications, such as blindness, kidney damage, cardiovascular disease, and lower-limb amputations, but people with diabetes can lower the occurrence of these and other diabetes complications by controlling blood glucose, blood pressure, and blood lipids.

- Many people with type 2 diabetes can control their blood glucose by following a healthy meal plan and exercise program, losing excess weight, and taking oral medication. Some people with type 2 diabetes may also need insulin to control their blood glucose.

- To survive, people with type 1 diabetes must have insulin delivered by injection or a pump.

- Among adults with diagnosed diabetes—type 1 or type 2—14 percent take insulin only, 13 percent take both insulin and oral medication, 57 percent take oral medication only, and 16 percent do not take either insulin or oral medication. Medications for each individual with diabetes will often change over the course of the disease.

- Many people with diabetes also need to take medications to control their cholesterol and blood pressure.

- Self-management education or training is a key step in improving health outcomes and quality of life. It focuses on self-care behaviors, such as healthy eating, being active, and monitoring blood glucose. It is a collaborative process in which diabetes educators help people with or at risk for diabetes gain the knowledge and problem-solving and coping skills needed to successfully self-manage the disease and its related conditions.

Pre-Diabetes

Pre-diabetes is a condition in which individuals have blood glucose levels higher than normal but not high enough to be classified as diabetes. People with pre-diabetes have an increased risk of developing type 2 diabetes, heart disease, and stroke.

- People with pre-diabetes have impaired fasting glucose (IFG) or impaired glucose tolerance (IGT). Some people have both IFG and IGT.

- IFG is a condition in which the fasting blood glucose level is 100 to 125 milligrams per deciliter (mg/dL) after an overnight fast. This level is higher than normal but not high enough to be classified as diabetes.

- IGT is a condition in which the blood glucose level is 140 to 199 mg/dL after a 2-hour oral glucose tolerance test. This level is higher than normal but not high enough to be classified as diabetes.

Prevention or Delay of Diabetes

- Progression to diabetes among those with pre-diabetes is not inevitable. Studies have shown that people with pre-diabetes who lose weight and increase their physical activity can prevent or delay diabetes and even return their blood glucose levels to normal.

- In the Diabetes Prevention Program, a large prevention study of people at high risk for diabetes, lifestyle intervention reduced the development of diabetes by 58 percent over 3 years. The reduction was even greater, 71 percent, among adults aged 60 years or older.

- Interventions to prevent or delay type 2 diabetes in individuals with pre-diabetes can be feasible and cost effective. Research has found that lifestyle interventions are more cost effective than medications.

Complications of Diabetes in the United States

- Adults with diabetes have heart-disease death rates about 2 to 4 times higher than adults without diabetes. The risk for stroke is 2 to 4 times higher among people with diabetes.

- In 2003 to 2004, 75 percent of adults with self-reported diabetes had blood pressure greater than or equal to 130/80 millimeters of mercury (mm Hg) or used prescription medications for hypertension.

- Diabetes is the leading cause of new cases of blindness among adults aged 20 to 74 years. Diabetic retinopathy causes 12,000 to 24,000 new cases of blindness each year.

- Diabetes is the leading cause of kidney failure.

- About 60 to 70 percent of people with diabetes have mild to severe forms of nervous system damage. The results of such damage include impaired sensation or pain in the feet or hands, slowed digestion of food in the stomach, carpal tunnel syndrome, erectile dysfunction, or other nerve problems. Almost 30 percent of people with diabetes aged 40 years or older have impaired sensation in the feet—for example, at least 1 area that lacks feeling. Severe forms of diabetic nerve disease are a major contributing cause of lower-extremity amputations.

- More than 60 percent of nontraumatic lower-limb amputations occur in people with diabetes.

- Periodontal, or gum, disease is more common in people with diabetes. Among young adults, those with diabetes have about twice the risk of those without diabetes. Persons with poorly controlled diabetes (A1C > 9 percent) were nearly 3 times more likely to have severe periodontitis than those without diabetes. Almost ⅓ of people with diabetes have severe periodontal disease with loss of attachment of the gums to the teeth measuring 5 millimeters or more.

- Poorly controlled diabetes before conception and during the first trimester of pregnancy among women with type 1 diabetes can cause major birth defects in 5 to 10 percent of pregnancies and spontaneous abortions in 15 to 20 percent of pregnancies. Poorly controlled diabetes during the second and third trimesters of pregnancy can result in excessively large babies, posing a risk to both mother and child.

- Uncontrolled diabetes often leads to biochemical imbalances that can cause acute life-threatening events, such as diabetic ketoacidosis and hyperosmolar, or nonketotic, coma. People with diabetes are more susceptible to many other illnesses and, once they acquire these illnesses, often have worse prognoses. For example, they are more likely to die from pneumonia or influenza than people who do not have diabetes. Persons with diabetes aged 60 years or older are 2 to 3 times more likely to report an inability to walk a quarter of a mile, climb stairs, do housework, or use a mobility aid compared with persons without diabetes in the same age group.

Preventing Diabetes Complications

Diabetes can affect many parts of the body and can lead to serious complications such as blindness, kidney damage, and lower-limb amputations. Working together, people with diabetes, their support network, and their healthcare providers can reduce the occurrence of these and other diabetes complications by controlling the levels of blood glucose, blood pressure, and blood lipids and by receiving other preventive care practices in a timely manner.

Glucose Control

- Studies in the United States and abroad have found that improved glycemic control benefits people with either type 1 or type 2 diabetes. In general, every percentage point drop in A1C blood-test results—for example, from 8 to 7 percent—can reduce the risk of microvascular complications—eye, kidney, and nerve diseases—by 40 percent.

- In patients with type 1 diabetes, intensive insulin therapy has long-term beneficial effects on the risk of cardiovascular disease.

Blood-Pressure Control

- Blood-pressure control reduces the risk of cardiovascular disease—heart disease or stroke—among persons with diabetes by 33 to 50 percent, and the risk of microvascular complications—eye, kidney, and nerve diseases—by approximately 33 percent.

- In general, for every 10 mm Hg reduction in systolic blood pressure, the risk for any complication related to diabetes is reduced by 12 percent.

Control of Blood Lipids

- Improved control of LDL cholesterol can reduce cardiovascular complications by 20 to 50 percent.

Preventive Care Practices for Eyes, Feet, and Kidneys

- Detecting and treating diabetic eye disease with laser therapy can reduce the development of severe vision loss by an estimated 50 to 60 percent.

- Comprehensive foot-care programs can reduce amputation rates by 45 to 85 percent.

- Detecting and treating early diabetic kidney disease by lowering blood pressure can reduce the decline in kidney function by 30 to 70 percent. Treatment with angiotensin-converting enzyme

(ACE) inhibitors and angiotensin receptor blockers (ARBs) are more effective in reducing the decline in kidney function than other blood-pressure-lowering drugs.

- In addition to lowering blood pressure, ARBs reduce proteinuria, a risk factor for developing kidney disease, by 35 percent—similar to the reduction achieved by ACE inhibitors.

Source: National Institutes of Health

The Pancreas

The pancreas is located high up in the abdomen. It is about the size and shape of a banana and sits behind the stomach. The pancreas is a gland organ and produces pancreatic digestive juices. It also produces insulin and other hormones related to digestion. Insulin helps to keep sugar in the blood at a stable level.

Nutrition, Diet, and Exercise

Up to 80 percent of type 2 diabetes is preventable by adopting a healthy diet and increasing activity. Glucose control is key to preventing or developing complications of diabetes.

What Should a Person with Diabetes Eat?

A person with diabetes should eat a healthy diet similar to the healthy diet recommended for the general population. This would include lean protein sources such as meats, fish, poultry, nuts, eggs, beans, and soy. These protein sources should be low in total fat, low in saturated fat, and contain no or very little trans fat. The diet should also include healthy carbohydrates with fiber such as fruits, vegetables, and healthy whole grains. Low-fat or fat-free calcium sources are also important to include, such as milk, cheese, yogurt, and soy products. Naturally, all food choices need to be portion controlled.

Proteins

Protein comes from meats, poultry, fish and seafood, beans and nuts, dairy foods, and grains. Three to 6 ounces a day is the recommended amount of lean protein in the diet. Good lean choices include most fish and seafood and skinless poultry such as chicken and turkey. Remember, there's about 5 times more fat in a piece of chicken with the skin on it compared to a skinless piece, so be sure to remove the skin. Use low-fat cooking methods for these foods, such as broiling, grilling, roasting, or baking, and trim excess fat beforehand or drain away the fat after cooking.

Eggs, beans, nuts, and soy are good protein sources, provided you exercise portion control. Beans, nuts, and soy provide heart-healthy fat benefits and also provide carbohydrates and fiber. It's important to remember when using canned beans—or any canned vegetables—to rinse in a strainer under cool running water, to remove about 40 percent of the sodium.

Milk, Cheese, and Yogurt

Select fat-free or 1 percent milk and dairy products whenever possible, with little or no added sugars. I prefer to buy whole milk and dilute it with an equal amount of water when cooking or baking in order to cut the carbs and the price of milk in half. You must realize, however, that this also cuts the nutrients such as calcium in half, if this is important to your diet. Dairy is a major source of calcium in our diets. It is recommended that children have 3-4 servings a day; adults need a minimum of 3. Fortified soy beverages are a good alternative for those who do not care for or are allergic to dairy.

Fruits and Vegetables

Recommendations are to eat at least 2 servings of fruits and 3-5 servings of vegetables a day. Fruits must be eaten in moderation, as calories and carbs can be high. Fruits and fruit juices should be unsweetened. Drain or rinse canned fruit. Fruit juices tend to spike blood glucose levels fast, so use in moderation and choose whole fruits over juices, as they contain fiber, are not as concentrated, and lead to lower spikes in blood glucose levels.

Most green vegetables are lower in carbohydrates and calories than other vegetables. These would include leafy green vegetables such as spinach, cabbage, Brussels sprouts, and greens as well as broccoli, celery, green beans, asparagus, artichokes, and peppers. All vegetables can be eaten, in moderation. Here again, canned vegetables should be rinsed before preparing. Potatoes and other vegetables should never be fried. Starchy vegetables such as potatoes and corn should be limited to ½ cup per serving. Cauliflower is lower in carbs and can be cooked and mashed with a little cream or milk in place of mashed potatoes. It can also be steamed and served in place of potatoes, rice, or pasta with your meals.

Grains

Grains include cereals, breads, rice, and pasta. They provide the body with carbohydrates for energy and also needed fiber. Whole grains are almost always the best choice: brown rice, whole oats, whole wheat, etc. Sourdough bread products may be tolerated very well by some individuals with diabetes. Personal testing is recommended. Many diabetics swear by the taste of Dreamfield's Whole Grain Pasta®. Dietary recommendations state that at least half of one's grain foods should be whole grains. Look for choices that do not contain added sugar, honey, or other sweeteners. Grain choices should contain a minimum of 3-4 grams a serving and should be portion controlled. A portion is 1 cup cereal, ½ cup cooked rice or pasta, or 1 ounce bread.

Oils and Spreads

Vegetable oils such as olive and canola oil are the healthiest choices for cooking and baking. Trans fats are to be severely limited.

Look for trans-fat-free shortening for baking. Some fat is necessary for good health, but make sure you are choosing heart-healthy fats whenever possible. Butter is fine in moderation—it should be used as a "discretionary food." My recipe for Canola Butter in chapter 4 is a healthier alternative.

Snacks and Sweets

Limit snacks and sweets and always use portion control. This includes sugar-free and low-fat products, as they can be high in carbs and calories. Fruits are a good alternative to sweets, because they provide fiber and nutrients. Baked chips and pretzels should be selected. The dessert recipes in this book typically provide healthier and tastier alternatives than those you would get elsewhere. They challenge you to utilize better ingredients for healthier outcomes.

Carb Counting

A meal-planning technique many diabetics use for managing their blood glucose levels is known as "carb counting." Carb counting should take into account how active you are and what, if any, medications you are taking. Generally diabetics should start with 45-60 grams of carbs per meal and adjust this according to their health. Food labels and carb counters can help in calculating carbs.

The Plate Method

The plate method is another technique for portioning meals. Visually divide your plate into 3 unequal sections. Half the plate should be filled with nonstarchy vegetables; a little over one-fourth with your protein source such as meat, seafood, or poultry; and the remainder with a starch and or whole grains such as bread or crackers. You can add to this an 8-oz. glass of milk and a piece of fruit.

Diets

There are many diets out there touted to be beneficial for diabetics. The Zone Diet, Atkins Diet, South Beach Diet, Raw Foods Diet, and Healthy Exchange Diet all come to mind. Many of these are limiting and monotonous. You'll notice that many of these diets seem to contradict each other, yet people are both helped and harmed by them all. The safest way to diet is to follow the advice of your personal physician or other licensed healthcare provider, while being monitored. Also remember that moderation with all foods is healthier for your body and sanity. Know that certain oral diabetes medications may result in significant weight gain and may need to be substituted by your physician with other more weight friendly, effective medications.

Supplements

Supplements that can be beneficial to diabetics include cinnamon and cinnamon capsules, alpha-lipoic acid, and chromium.

Exercise

To maintain normal blood glucose levels, a combination of aerobic, strength-training, and flexibility exercises is recommended for 30 minutes a day, at least 5 days a week. If you're trying to lose weight, you may want to exceed 30 minutes a day. My favorite indoor exercise is stepping or marching to dance music while swinging my arms.

Chapter 2

Flours

kes

My motive for writing this book is to share my method of baking delicious, homemade, diabetic-friendly desserts and to make it easy for my readers to do the same. So here I am providing the key points I use as the basis to transform just about any dessert recipe to one that bodes well for my blood sugar and taste buds. I'm hoping you can use these key points to do the same. Don't be afraid to experiment. Go through your old cookbooks and recipe cards, and turn your old favorites into new diabetic-friendly versions.

Wheat Flours

White flour has most of the wheat bran and wheat germ extracted. White flour comes in bleached and unbleached varieties. The unbleached flour has a creamy color. Bleached flour is whitened by treating with flour-bleaching agents. All-purpose flour is a blended white flour of medium strength that works well in most baked goods.

Bread flour is a white flour considered to be strong, derived from wheat that is high in protein, though not as high as in whole-wheat equivalents.

Cake flour, also known as white pastry flour, is a white flour that has been milled very finely from soft wheat. It has very low gluten strength, making it suitable for soft-textured cookies and cakes such as sponge cakes. Higher gluten would make these products tough. Cake flour should not be used in breads, most cookies, quick breads, muffins, or biscuits, as they tend to become too crumbly.

Whole-wheat flour, made from red wheat, is milled from the whole grain (bran, germ, and endosperm). Nothing is added or taken away. It is brown in color and somewhat coarse. If the flour is organic, it is milled from organic wheat that is produced without the use of artificial fertilizers or pesticides. Whole-wheat flour is more nutritious than refined white flour and more suitable for diabetics, as whole grains are more slowly absorbed in the body, resulting in lower blood-sugar spikes. Whole-wheat flour has a shorter shelf life than white flour, but its shelf life can be lengthened by refrigerating or freezing. Whole-wheat flour does not rise as well as white flour, which can make baked goods heavier. For best baking results, it is advisable to mix it with white or some other flour. A bit more liquid may need to be added as well.

White whole-wheat flour is produced from soft white wheat varieties. It has a lighter color, milder flavor, and finer texture than whole-wheat flour. I like to think of it as a cross between white and whole-wheat flours. It can replace all-purpose flour cup for cup in cookies, muffins, quick breads, and pancakes. There are differences in the brands of white whole-wheat flour. I find the King Arthur® brand of white whole-wheat flour to be superior for baking, as the color is lighter and it is milled finer than most other brands I've tried.

Whole-wheat pastry flour is milled from low-protein soft wheat. It is typically used in cookies, piecrusts, and hearty cakes. It is similar to white pastry flour, but not all of the bran and germ portions of the wheat kernel have been removed during milling. It is fine textured and has a high starch content. Whole-wheat pastry flour is more nutritious than white pastry flour, but finished products are not as light and airy. This flour works well in delicate baked goods and in piecrusts.

Graham flour is a type of whole-wheat flour but it is bleached and less processed. It is good for making graham crackers and quick breads. It can be substituted for whole-wheat flour in recipes.

Other Flours

Oat flour is milled from oats and can be easily made at home by grinding old-fashioned or quick oats in a blender or food processor until fine and powdery. It is good in breads, quick breads, and piecrusts.

Soy flour is milled from roasted soybeans. It does not contain gluten so cannot completely replace wheat flour in a recipe. It is recommended to replace only ¼ of any wheat flour with a bean flour in your recipes. Other bean flours to experiment with include white bean and fava bean. Most beans are milled into flours, but some, such as soy, have strong flavors, so use those judiciously. I also find that soy flour has a tendency to stick to pans and griddles if they are not greased sufficiently. You may love it. It's all a matter of preference.

Almond flour can easily be made by grinding blanched (no skin) almonds in your blender or food processor until fine, but before they turn into butter. Nut flours are lower in carbs. Almond flour is generally made with blanched almonds and almond meal with either whole or blanched almonds. Almond flour or meal is good in cakes, tortes, and quick breads. Almond flour does not work well in yeasted breads. It makes a great substitute for flour and has a good flavor but is expensive. Most nuts can be ground for use as flour. Nut flours do not contain gluten so do not rise well. Try substituting ¼ of wheat flour with nut flour.

Coconut flour is a low-carb, gluten-free flour that is high in fiber and protein. It is made from finely ground coconut meat that has been defatted. Generally coconut flour cannot completely replace wheat flour, as it contains no gluten. However, if you add 1 egg per 1 oz. coconut flour in your recipe, it can be a 100 percent substitute for wheat flour. Otherwise, try substituting 15 to 25 percent coconut flour in your baked goods. It can be used in cakes, pies, and breads.

Buckwheat flour has a stronger flavor than wheat flour and can be described as rich and nutty. It is good in breads, muffins, pancakes, and biscuits. It is recommended to replace up to ⅕ of the wheat flour in recipes, except for buckwheat pancakes. Buckwheat flour is good in breads, muffins, pancakes, and biscuits.

Barley flour has a mild, nutty flavor. It can replace ¼ of wheat flour in a recipe containing yeast and ½ in other baked goods. Barley flour is good in cookies, pancakes, and quick breads.

Quinoa flour (pronounced *keen*-wah) has a pleasant nutty flavor. It has a higher fat content than wheat flour, which makes baked goods moister. It is gluten free and good in breads, biscuits, cookies, muffins, pancakes, tortillas, and crepes. Replace up to ¼ wheat flour in bread recipes with quinoa flour.

Spelt flour is nutty in flavor but also slightly sweet. It contains gluten. Spelt is a bit heavy, so you can replace whole-wheat flours in bread. It can also be blended with wheat flour and is good in all types of breads, cookies, and muffins.

Brown rice flour is milled from unpolished brown rice. It has a slightly grainy texture and is gluten free. The flour should be refrigerated to keep it from going rancid quickly. Brown rice flour has a nutty flavor. It does not rise well in yeast breads. It can be combined with other flours to be used in baking. It works well in breads, cookies, cakes, and pastries. Replace up to ¼ of any flour with this.

Amaranth flour is a high-protein, high-fiber, gluten-free flour with a unique flavor. It can be used to replace ¼ of the flour in your recipes. It goes well in quick breads and cookies.

Flaxseed flour has a high nutrient value and good flavor. It enhances the flavor of recipes containing whole wheat. You can substitute ¼ of the flour in almost any baking recipe with flaxseed flour, although the baked goods will brown more easily. Because of its oil content, it can be substituted for all or some of the fat, depending on the recipe. You can substitute 3 tbsp. ground flaxseed for 1 tbsp. butter or vegetable oil.

Wheat germ contains 23 nutrients. It is a byproduct of the milling of wheat and has more nutrients per ounce than any other vegetable or grain. It is also high in fiber. Therefore, it is generally added to recipes to boost the nutritional value. You can replace up to ⅓ of the flour in your breads and quick breads with wheat germ.

Wheat bran is a byproduct of wheat and has proven to be highly nutritious. It can be added to breads, quick breads, and cookies. Wheat bran should be stored in the refrigerator to prevent it from going rancid. It is generally used in baked goods to increase fiber and nutrients. It can be substituted for ⅓ of the flour in many recipes. As bran absorbs more liquid than flour, it should be combined with wet ingredients and allowed to set a few minutes to allow the bran to absorb the moisture.

Oat bran is the outer husk of the oat grain. It is high in fiber and contains many minerals. Oats reduce blood glucose and insulin responses. Oat bran is used in muffins, pancakes, scones, and some cookies. You can substitute up to ⅓ of the flour in your recipes with oat bran.

Rye flour is milled from whole rye berries and grains of rye grass. It is high in bran and soluble fiber, has a very low gluten content, and is usually blended with wheat flour—no more than ⅓ cup rye flour per 1 cup wheat flour.

Flour Mixtures

I find that most pastry recipes work best when some white flour is used. My favorite flour mixture consists of 1 part all-purpose flour, 1 part white whole-wheat flour, 1 part soy flour, and 1 part oat flour. I use this in muffins, waffles, coffeecakes, and quick breads. I find that this mixture does not raise my blood glucose levels. I urge you to experiment to come up with mixtures that suit your own taste, texture, and health requirements.

My second favorite flour mixture is 1 part white flour and 1 part white whole-wheat flour. This works well in most recipes. The King Arthur® brand of white whole-wheat flour mimics the color, taste, and texture of white flour more closely than any other brand I've tested, resulting in the best approximation of traditional baked goods.

My favorite flour mixture for cakes is 1 part cake flour and 1 part King Arthur® white whole-wheat flour or whole-wheat pastry flour. Pound cakes also turn out well using 1 part whole-wheat pastry flour and 1 part bread flour.

Piecrusts can benefit from whole-wheat pastry flour or 1 part all-purpose flour to 1 part whole-wheat pastry flour.

I don't always make the recipes in this book the same way. Depending on my mood, I will use different combinations of flours. I use these recipes simply as a guideline.

If carb counting is extremely important to you, you might want to experiment by using or mixing some of the lower-carb flours such as coconut, almond, soy, oat, or flaxseed. Wheat germ, wheat bran, and oat bran are also low carb and can be used for extra nutrition. Use your imagination and taste buds to come up with winning low-carb combinations for your signature dishes.

Chapter 3

Sugar and Sugar Substitutes

Sugar

Sugar is a crystalline carbohydrate and is created naturally in all fruits and vegetables. It adds sweetness and flavor to foods, and in baking it provides bulk, structure, caramelization, and moistness. Excessive consumption of sugar has been associated with increased incidences of type 2 diabetes, obesity, and tooth decay.

My General Rules for Baking with Sugar

- Typical muffin recipes should contain no more than ¼ cup sugar. Splenda® is not recommended.

- Coffee cakes should contain no more than 1 cup sugar. Splenda® is not recommended.

- Pound cakes should typically contain no more than 1½ cups sugar. Additional sweetening should come from Splenda®.

- Layer cakes are best made by reducing the sugar in the recipe. Splenda® is not recommended.

- Tea breads are best made by reducing the sugar in the recipe. Splenda® is not recommended.

- Fruit pies can be made with no added sugar. Splenda® can replace the sugar.

- Puddings and custards can be made with no sugar. They are typically better, however, with some added sugar.

- Cheesecakes can be made with no added sugar. Splenda® can replace the sugar.

Sugar Substitutes

A sugar substitute is a food additive that duplicates the taste of sugar but usually has less food energy. People with diabetes have difficulty regulating their blood sugar levels. With artificial sweeteners, they can enjoy a varied diet while closely controlling their sugar intake.

Splenda®

Splenda® is a no-calorie sweetener that can be enjoyed by the whole family. Splenda® is a sucralose sweetener, a chlorinated sugar that is about 600 times sweeter than sugar. It is produced from sucrose (sugar) when 3 chlorine atoms are genetically altered to replace 3 hydroxyl groups. Because of this, its famous slogan— "Splenda® is made from sugar, so it tastes like sugar"—has come under fire not for the safety of the product but for its marketing, which is considered to be a bit misleading.

My experience shows that Splenda® works best in fruit pies, cheesecakes, shortbread and gingerbread cookies, jams and jellies, frozen desserts, puddings and custards, mousses, sauces, fruit sweetening, and beverages. In recipes such as angel food cakes, meringues, and pound cakes, an equal amount of sugar is generally necessary to provide structure.

I find for most muffins, cakes, and cookies it is better to lessen the amount of sugar rather than use Splenda®. But having said that, there are exceptions, and I urge you to experiment some yourself to see what is acceptable to your own taste buds and blood sugar levels. Despite its limitations, Splenda® is currently the most popular sugar substitute on the market and considered to be the best major sugar substitute for baking. Splenda® can be recognized by its yellow packaging.

Other points to keep in mind when baking with Splenda®:

- If you do use Splenda® when baking cookies, they may not spread and may need to be flattened before baking.

- Your batter will look different when you cream Splenda® with butter and add your eggs. The final product will be okay, but if this bothers you, add your Splenda® to your other dry ingredients, and do not cream with butter or other fats.

- Splenda® will not activate yeast.

- Splenda® will not caramelize like sugar. To compensate for this, you can try spraying your baked goods with cooking spray before baking.

- In cookie recipes that call for both brown and white sugar, replace the white sugar with Splenda®, but include the brown sugar that is called for. Brown sugar is used not only for flavor and color but also to make cookies chewy or crunchy.

- To enhance the flavor of cookies, puddings, and custards, you may want to add 1 tsp. vanilla extract.

- Custards and puddings made with Splenda® may be a bit thinner in consistency. A bit of cornstarch generally helps.

- Baked goods do not rise as high with Splenda®. If you're baking cakes, you may want to use a pan a bit smaller than called for to counter this.

- If you decide to use Splenda® in your quick breads and muffins, add 1-2 tbsp. honey or molasses to boost the flavor and add moistness.

- Baked goods made with Splenda® typically brown a bit faster. Cakes may be done up to 10 min. sooner, muffins 5-8 min. sooner, and cookies 3-5 min. sooner. So keep checking your oven!

- Baked goods made with Splenda® tend to be drier and don't store as well at room temperature. It's best to refrigerate most of these products. Baked goods made with Splenda® freeze well.

Sweet'N Low®

Sweet'N Low® is the brand name of an artificial sweetener known as saccharin. Sweet'N Low® was invented in 1879 and marketed early in the 20th century as a sugar substitute for diabetics. Because of its bitter aftertaste, it has been mostly replaced by sucralose and aspartame. It is still, however, commonly used to sweeten beverages. Sweet'N Low® is heat stable, but it is rarely used in baking. Saccharin is 200-700 times sweeter than sugar. For years saccharin was thought to cause cancer in humans, as large amounts were shown to cause bladder cancer in male rats. However, in 2000, saccharin was removed from the list of cancer-causing substances. It was determined that the risk was not relative to human biology, and warning labels were removed from Sweet'N Low®'s widely recognized pink packaging.

Equal®

Equal® is a brand of artificial sweetener containing aspartame, dextrose, and maltodextrin. It is marketed by a company that also owns NutraSweet®, which is also aspartame. Aspartame is 160-220 times sweeter than sugar. Since it loses its sweetening power when heated, it is not suitable for baking cakes and cookies. Equal® and NutraSweet® can be recognized by their blue packaging.

Sugar Alcohols

Sugar alcohols are a hydrogenated form of carbohydrate used in many commercial food products in place of table sugar (sucrose). Part of their structure resembles sugar and part resembles alcohol. Sugar alcohols are usually not completely absorbed into the bloodstream from the small intestines, minimizing spikes in blood glucose levels. Overconsumption of sugar alcohols can lead to severe stomach upset. However. with continued use, many people develop a degree of tolerance to sugar alcohols. Read your food labels. Most sugar alcohols end in *-ol,* such as sorbitol, glycol, maltitol, and erythritol. There are many different names for sugar alcohols. Two that do not end in *-ol* are isomalt and HSH. Intolerance to sugar alcohols is a good reason to bake your own homemade desserts.

Stevia

Stevia is a natural herb of the sunflower family, native to South and Central America. It is significantly sweeter than sugar and generally available through health-food stores and natural-food grocery stores. Stevia was previously banned from use as a sweetener in the U.S. It is beginning to gain consumer acceptance. Stevia is heat stable and suitable for cooking and baking. Stevia is said not to raise blood glucose levels. It is available in both liquid and powdered forms and light and dark varieties. Stevia has a slightly bitter aftertaste resembling licorice. It is commercially packaged in grocery stores under the name Truvia®.

Agave Nectar

Agave nectar is a natural sweetener derived from the agave plant and commercially produced in Mexico. It is a nectar concentrated to a syruplike liquid and often substituted for honey in recipes. It is similar in taste and consistency to honey, though a bit thinner. It is also used to sweeten beverages and can be poured straight out of the bottle as a syrup for pancakes or waffles. Agave nectar is best known as the plant from which tequila is made. It does not have the aftertaste associated with artificial sweeteners. It is sold in light and dark varieties. Agave nectar has a low glycemic index and glycemic load and can be used safely by some diabetics.

Whey Low®

Whey Low® is a natural sweetener developed in the U.S. with a glycemic index 70-80 percent lower than sugar. It can be used as a complete replacement for sugar in all foods. It is suitable for cooking and baking. Whey Low® Granular contains fructose, lactose, and sucrose and is said to be suitable for diabetics who already have tight control of their blood glucose levels and do not overindulge in sweets. Whey Low® Type D is a blend of fructose and lactose and said to be ideal for type 1 and type 2 diabetics. Baking with Whey Low® Type D requires a 10-degree drop in temperature and a longer bake time. Whey Low® is advertised as tasting exactly like sugar.

Chapter 4

Hints and Tips

Portion Size

Portion size matters. If you've ever found yourself baking a cake or pie and devouring it all in a few sittings, this tip is for you. Think portion size. Don't bake a cake—bake cupcakes, or bake your pound cake batter in mini cake pans. Eat one and freeze the remainder of the individual portions. Don't bake a pie—bake small tarts. Portion puddings and ice cream into ramekins. One or 2 cookies is a portion size. Freeze the rest. Once you've had your portion for the day, that's it.

Cinnamon

Try adding cinnamon to your waffles, muffins, pancakes, quick breads, baked fruit pies, and other baked goods. One-half tsp. cinnamon per day has been shown to lower blood glucose levels by up to 20 percent in some individuals. Drink cinnamon tea with your desserts.

Cost Cutters

Diabetes is an expensive disease. *The Diabetic Pastry Chef* method of baking is designed to not only keep your blood glucose levels in check but also save you money. Splenda® for baking is expensive. You can cut costs by mixing sugar with Splenda® yourself. It also saves you money to make your own canola butter and buy whole milk and mix it with an equal part of water to cook and bake with. Diluting milk this way cuts its carbs in half. You can do the same with whole buttermilk.

Baking Powder

2 tbsp. cream of tartar
1 tbsp. baking soda
1 tbsp. cornstarch

Sift ingredients together and mix well. Store in an airtight container.

Tip for Fruit Pies and Crisps

When making fruit pies and crisps, add ¼-½ tsp. baking soda to neutralize the acid content. Then you will only need to add half the amount of sugar the recipe calls for. The finished product will taste as sweet as if you used the full amount of sugar.

Unsuccessful Recipes

Unsuccessful cakes and cookies can be turned into successful parfaits and trifles. Stale cakes and cookies can be used the same way. Simply crumble and layer with sugar-free pudding and whipped cream. A little liqueur and fruit can be added, if you'd like.

Egg Substitutions

In baking, you may use 1 heaping tbsp. soy flour and 1 tbsp. water to equal 1 egg. There is no texture or taste difference in the finished product. Occasionally, substitute "some" of the whole eggs in a recipe with soy flour or egg whites (consider this when a recipe calls for more than 2 eggs). Below are some other substitution options.

1 large egg = 1½ large egg whites
1 large egg = 3 tbsp. egg substitute

1 large egg = 1 large egg white + 2 tsp. canola oil (to reduce the cholesterol)
1 large egg white = 2 tbsp. egg substitute

Replacing Solid Fats with Canola Oil

If a recipe calls for oil, I always use canola oil as a healthy choice. You can also replace butter, shortening, or margarine from your favorite recipes with canola oil by using the following chart. This will make most of your baked goods moist with a soft texture. Therefore, if you want to make a cookie with a crisp texture, do not replace.

1 cup solid fat = ¾ cup canola oil
¾ cup solid fat = ⅔ cup canola oil
½ cup solid fat = ⅓ cup canola oil
¼ cup solid fat = 3 tbsp. canola oil

Canola Butter or Olive Butter

2 cups butter, softened
1½ cups canola oil or olive oil

Whip butter with electric mixer. Add oil and beat. Pour into container and refrigerate until hardened. Keep refrigerated. Yield: 3½ cups.

Use this as a healthy spread for quick breads, biscuits, waffles, and muffins and to butter vegetables.

Use anywhere you would use butter or margarine. It works well in most recipes that call for butter, margarine, shortening, or Smart Balance® regular spread.

Nutrition Facts		
Amount Per Total Recipe		
Calories 6,146 (100% from Fat, 0% from Protein, 0% from Carb)		
Total Fat 695 g		
Saturated Fat 256 g		
Mono Fat 288 g		
Cholesterol 976 mg		
Sodium 2615 mg		
Total Carbohydrate 0 g		
Dietary Fiber 0 g		
Sugars 0 g		
Protein 4 g		
Calcium 109 mg		
Iron 0 mg		

Dough Enhancer

Dough enhancer improves the texture and increases the shelf life of baked goods. Add it to pizza dough, cakes, scones, rolls, and breads—especially whole-wheat breads. However, if you want a traditional chewy bread and crisp crust, do not add it to sourdough recipes.

Cakes

I find pound cakes and angel food cakes to be preferable to layer cakes, as they do not require icing.

Reduced-Sugar Cake Mixes

Reduced-sugar cake mixes may have less sugar but the same amount of carbs as regular cake mixes. Therefore, they may not be as beneficial as they are touted to be.

Sugar-Free Sweetened Condensed Milk

1 (12 oz.) can evaporated skim milk
1½ cups nonfat dry milk powder
½ cup Splenda®

In large bowl, combine all ingredients thoroughly. Refrigerate. Will keep for up to 1 week. Yield: 3½ cups.

Nutrition Facts	
Amount Per Total Recipe	
Calories 965 (2% from Fat, 38% from Protein, 60% from Carb)	
Total Fat 2 g	
Saturated Fat 1 g	
Mono Fat 1 g	
Cholesterol 50 mg	
Sodium 1354 mg	
Total Carbohydrate 144 g	
Dietary Fiber 0 g	
Sugars 132 g	
Protein 91 g	
Calcium 3249 mg	
Iron 2 mg	

Sweetened Whipped Cream

1 cup whipping cream, thoroughly chilled
2-3 tbsp. Splenda®
½ tsp. vanilla extract

Beat all ingredients in bowl with mixer until cream thickens and soft peaks form. Yield: 2 cups.

Nutrition Facts
Amount Per Total Recipe
Calories 369 (90% from Fat, 3% from Protein, 7% from Carb)
Total Fat 37 g
Saturated Fat 23 g
Mono Fat 11 g
Cholesterol 133 mg
Sodium 41 mg
Total Carbohydrate 7 g
Dietary Fiber 0 g
Sugars 0 g
Protein 3 g
Calcium 83 mg
Iron 0 mg

Powdered Sugar

¾ cup regular Splenda®
2 tbsp. cornstarch

Place in blender and blend to a fine powder. Use in recipes calling for powdered or confectioners' sugar.

Yogurt Tip

Plain yogurt can be substituted for an equal amount of sour cream in most of your baked goods. You can also substitute plain yogurt for the oil and eggs in packaged brownie mixes to save 119 grams fat and 424 milligrams cholesterol per batch. Add ½ cup plain yogurt and the amount of water called for. Bake approximately 30 min. at 350 degrees.

Applesauce Tip

If you substitute unsweetened applesauce for an equal amount of oil in your yellow or white packaged cake mixes, you will save 73 grams fat and 642 calories. The cake will keep best in the refrigerator. You can prepare breads and muffins the same way. One-half cup unsweetened applesauce only has 9 grams sugar.

Fat-Free Cream Cheese

Fat-free cream cheese may work well for spreads but not for recipes where beating or baking is required, as it does not melt well. It is better to use full-fat or reduced-fat cream cheese in baking.

Flaxseed

Ground flaxseed can be substituted for fat in a recipe. When flaxseed is used in place of oil, baked goods tend to brown more quickly.

3 tbsp. ground flaxseed = 1 tbsp. butter, margarine, or oil

Flaxseed can also be substituted for eggs. The finished product will be a little chewier.

1 tbsp. ground flaxseed + 3 tbsp. water = 1 egg

Flour

When adding a heavy flour such as whole-wheat flour to your recipes, you may have to add a tad more liquid to your recipe if your batter seems a bit dry.

Sugar-Free Oatmeal Cookies

You may take any oatmeal cookie recipe and substitute ½ box raisins that you have pulverized in a food processor or blender for the sugar. The remaining raisins can be added whole to your recipe.

Chapter 5

Breakfast and Brunch

A good breakfast puts me in a good mood for the rest of the day. I love being creative with breakfast. I can fix eggs a thousand ways—scrambled with cheese, scrambled with cream cheese, scrambled with cottage cheese, fried over easy, sunnyside up, poached, omelet, etc. But none of that matters if I don't have my hearty, whole-grain quick breads to serve alongside. Whole grains are perfect for breakfast. Here they can strut their stuff and be proud in pancakes, waffles, coffeecakes, scones, muffins, and biscuits. Mix your grains to your heart's content. Breakfast is served!

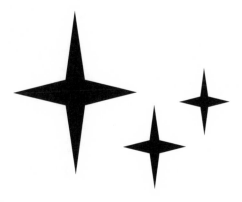

Baked Oatmeal Cereal

1 egg, lightly beaten
1½ cups rolled oats
½ cup Splenda®
½ cup milk
¼ cup canola oil
¼ cup chopped pecans or walnuts or sliced almonds
¼ cup raisins or dried cranberries
1 tsp. baking powder
½ tsp. salt
½ tsp. cinnamon

Combine well all ingredients and spread in a greased 8-in. square baking dish. Bake 25-30 min. at 350 degrees. The baked oatmeal will be firm but moist; it is not meant to be crispy. Cut into squares or scoop or spoon into bowls or small custard dishes. Serve hot with milk, a dab of Canola Butter (see index), and a bit of Splenda®. Refrigerate and microwave any leftovers.

I sometimes add a chopped apple to the mix before baking. I especially like using dried cranberries and sliced almonds in this dish! Yield: 6 servings.

Nutrition Facts
Amount Per Serving
Calories 489 (66% from Fat, 25% from Protein, 9% from Carb)
Total Fat 36 g
Saturated Fat 8 g
Mono Fat 16 g
Cholesterol 984 mg
Sodium 608 mg
Total Carbohydrate 11 g
Dietary Fiber 1 g
Sugars 7 g
Protein 30 g
Calcium 189 mg
Iron 5 mg

Cinnamon French Toast

2 eggs
½ cup milk
1 tbsp. sugar or Splenda®
½ tsp. cinnamon
Dash nutmeg
1 tsp. vanilla extract
6 slices day-old whole-wheat, sourdough, or oatmeal bread
Canola Butter (see index)
Sugar-free syrup

Beat together eggs, milk, sugar or Splenda®, cinnamon, nutmeg, and vanilla. Soak bread for 30 seconds on each side. Cook bread on a greased griddle until brown on each side. Serve hot with butter and syrup. Yield: 6 servings.

Nutrition Facts

Amount Per Serving

Calories 110 (26% from Fat, 19% from Protein, 55% from Carb)

Total Fat 3 g

  Saturated Fat 1 g

  Mono Fat 1 g

Cholesterol 83 mg

Sodium 166 mg

Total Carbohydrate 15 g

  Dietary Fiber 1 g

  Sugars 4 g

Protein 5 g

Calcium 54 mg

Iron 1 mg

My Favorite Pancakes

½ cup wheat germ
1 cup white flour
1 cup whole-wheat or white whole-wheat flour
2 tsp. baking powder
1 tbsp. Splenda® or sugar
1 tsp. salt
2 large eggs
3 cups milk
2 tbsp. canola oil
Canola Butter (see index)
Sugar-free syrup

In large bowl, mix together dry ingredients. In separate bowl, mix together wet ingredients. Add wet ingredients to dry ingredients and mix quickly.

Cook pancakes by dropping ¼ cup at a time onto a greased, preheated griddle. Turn when bubbles form and edges start to dry. Serve hot with butter and syrup. Yield: 18 servings.

Note: You may use all whole-wheat or white whole-wheat flour in this recipe, if desired.

Nutrition Facts

Amount Per Serving

Calories 97 (28% from Fat, 16% from Protein, 56% from Carb)

Total Fat 3 g	
Saturated Fat 1 g	
Mono Fat 1 g	
Cholesterol 29 mg	
Sodium 207 mg	
Total Carbohydrate 14 g	
Dietary Fiber 1 g	
Sugars 1 g	
Protein 4 g	
Calcium 66 mg	
Iron 1 mg	

Oatmeal Breakfast Pancakes

1 cup sifted whole-wheat pastry or whole-wheat regular flour
1 cup rolled oats
½ tsp. salt
2½ tsp. baking powder
1½ cups milk
1 egg
2 tbsp. canola oil or melted butter
Canola Butter (see index)
Sugar-free syrup

Mix together dry ingredients, add wet ingredients, and stir or whisk. Drop ¼ cupful at a time onto a lightly greased, preheated griddle. Cook until top of pancake is covered with bubbles and edges start to dry. Turn and cook other side. Serve hot with butter and syrup. Yield: 10-12 servings.

Nutrition Facts		
Amount Per Serving		
Calories 135 (29% from Fat, 14% from Protein, 58% from Carb)		
Total Fat 4 g		
Saturated Fat 1 g		
Mono Fat 2 g		
Cholesterol 22 mg		
Sodium 213 mg		
Total Carbohydrate 20 g		
Dietary Fiber 3 g		
Sugars 1 g		
Protein 5 g		
Calcium 88 mg		
Iron 2 mg		

Whole-Wheat Pancakes

1 cup whole-wheat pastry flour
½ tsp. baking soda
¼ tsp. salt
1 egg
1 cup buttermilk
2 tbsp. canola oil
Canola Butter (see index)
Sugar-free syrup

Sift dry ingredients, add wet ingredients, and whisk just until combined. Do not overmix. Drop ¼ cupful at a time onto a griddle or skillet that contains a small amount of heated oil. Turn when bubbles begin to form and edges start to dry. Serve hot with butter and syrup. Yield: 4 servings.

The original recipe called for white flour, ½ tsp. salt, and 2 tbsp. melted butter. I sometimes mix ½ cup white flour and ½ cup whole-wheat flour to make these.

Do not double this recipe. Make additional batches if necessary.

Nutrition Facts		
Amount Per Serving		
Calories 195 (40% from Fat, 14% from Protein, 46% from Carb)		
Total Fat 9 g		
Saturated Fat 1 g		
Mono Fat 5 g		
Cholesterol 63 mg		
Sodium 359 mg		
Total Carbohydrate 23 g		
Dietary Fiber 4 g		
Sugars 2 g		
Protein 7 g		
Calcium 54 mg		
Iron 1 mg		

Finnish Pancake

4 eggs
2 cups milk
¼ tsp. salt
2 tbsp. sugar
¼ cup white flour
¼ cup white whole-wheat flour
4 tbsp. butter, melted
Canola Butter (see index)
Sugar-free syrup

Combine all ingredients except butter, and mix with electric mixer or blender. Pour melted butter in an 8-in. square glass pan. Pour batter on top of melted butter. Spread to cover. Bake 30 min. in a preheated 350-degree oven. Garnish with fresh fruit and mint leaves, and serve hot with butter and syrup. Goes well with bacon or sausage. Yield: 8 servings.

Nutrition Facts

Amount Per Serving

Calories 148 (56% from Fat, 16% from Protein, 28% from Carb)

Total Fat 9 g	
Saturated Fat 5 g	
Mono Fat 3 g	
Cholesterol 140 mg	
Sodium 174 mg	
Total Carbohydrate 11 g	
Dietary Fiber 1 g	
Sugars 5 g	
Protein 6 g	
Calcium 64 mg	
Iron 1 mg	

Pop-Up Pancakes

½ cup milk
¼ cup white flour
¼ cup white whole-wheat flour
¼ tsp. cinnamon
½ tsp. vanilla extract
3 eggs
2 tbsp. butter, melted
Dash salt

Put all ingredients in blender and blend until smooth. Fill greased muffin-tin cavities about ⅓ full. Bake approximately 15-20 min. in a preheated 400-degree oven or until puffed and golden brown. Remove from oven. Pancakes will deflate. Remove immediately from muffin tin with knife. On top of each pancake, place a little Canola Butter (see index), sliced fruit or berries of your choice, and a sprinkling of Splenda® or powdered sugar. Serve hot with sugar-free syrup. Yield: 24 servings.

Note: This recipe can also be made using ½ cup whole-wheat pastry flour. Use your imagination for toppings. Canned apple-pie filling makes a good one. Also good topped with sour cream instead of butter.

Nutrition Facts

Amount Per Serving

Calories 29 (54% from Fat, 18% from Protein, 28% from Carb)

Total Fat 2 g	
Saturated Fat 1 g	
Mono Fat 1 g	
Cholesterol 33 mg	
Sodium 19 mg	
Total Carbohydrate 2 g	
Dietary Fiber 0 g	
Sugars 0 g	
Protein 1 g	
Calcium 9 mg	
Iron 0 mg	

Gingerbread Pancakes

¾ cup white flour

¾ cup white whole-wheat or oat flour

1 tbsp. baking powder

1 tsp. ginger

1 tsp. cinnamon

¼ tsp. cloves

¼ tsp. nutmeg

¼ tsp. salt

1¼ cups milk

1 egg

¼ cup dark molasses

2 tbsp. canola oil

In mixing bowl, mix together dry ingredients. In separate bowl, mix together wet ingredients. Add wet ingredients to dry ingredients and whisk well.

Drop pancakes ¼ cupful at a time onto hot, greased griddle. Turn when bubbles begin to form and edges start to dry. Serve hot with Canola Butter (see index) and sugar-free syrup. Yield: 12 servings.

Nutrition Facts		
Amount Per Serving		
Calories 109 (27% from Fat, 12% from Protein, 62% from Carb)		
Total Fat 3 g		
Saturated Fat 1 g		
Mono Fat 2 g		
Cholesterol 22 mg		
Sodium 190 mg		
Total Carbohydrate 18 g		
Dietary Fiber 2 g		
Sugars 5 g		
Protein 3 g		
Calcium 114 mg		
Iron 1 mg		

Cinnamon Pancakes

¾ cup white flour

½ cup white whole-wheat flour

2½ tsp. baking powder

2 tbsp. Splenda®

1 tsp. cinnamon

¾ tsp. salt

1 egg

1¼ cups milk

3 tbsp. canola oil

1 tsp. vanilla extract

In large bowl, sift together dry ingredients. In separate bowl, mix together wet ingredients. Slowly stir wet ingredients into dry ingredients, mixing only until dry ingredients are wet.

Drop pancakes onto hot, greased griddle ¼ cupful at a time. Turn when bubbles begin to form and edges start to dry. Serve hot with Canola Butter (see index) and sugar-free syrup. Yield: 12 servings.

Note: For thicker pancakes, use ¾ cup milk. For plain pancakes, omit cinnamon and vanilla.

Nutrition Facts
Amount Per Serving
Calories 93 (42% from Fat, 11% from Protein, 47% from Carb)
Total Fat 4 g
Saturated Fat 1 g
Mono Fat 2 g
Cholesterol 21 mg
Sodium 264 mg
Total Carbohydrate 11 g
Dietary Fiber 1 g
Sugars 1 g
Protein 3 g
Calcium 83 mg
Iron 1 mg

Whole-Grain Waffles

½ cup whole-wheat flour

½ cup white flour

½ cup soy flour

½ cup oat flour

1 tbsp. Splenda®

1 tsp. baking soda

½ tsp. baking powder

½ tsp. salt

2 eggs

2 cups buttermilk or sour milk* or combination

1 tbsp. vanilla extract

2 tbsp. canola oil

In large bowl, combine dry ingredients. In smaller bowl, combine wet ingredients. Add wet ingredients to dry ingredients and whisk just until mixed. Bake in preheated waffle iron according to manufacturer's directions until golden brown. Serve hot with Canola Butter (see index) and sugar-free syrup. Yield: 6 servings.

Note: This recipe also works well with whole-wheat pastry flour in lieu of the other flours. The waffles make great breakfast sandwiches with bacon, eggs, and cheese between them. A fun afternoon snack can be made by cutting the waffles into sticks and spreading with peanut butter.

*Milk can be soured by adding 2 tbsp. vinegar or fresh lemon juice to 2 cups whole milk. Stir, and let sit 5-10 min.

Nutrition Facts
Amount Per Serving
Calories 245 (35% from Fat, 18% from Protein, 47% from Carb)
Total Fat 9 g
Saturated Fat 2 g
Mono Fat 4 g
Cholesterol 83 mg
Sodium 519 mg
Total Carbohydrate 29 g
Dietary Fiber 4 g
Sugars 3 g
Protein 11 g
Calcium 107 mg
Iron 2 mg

Banana Waffles

¼ cup white flour

¼ cup soy flour

¼ cup oat flour

¼ cup whole-wheat or white whole-wheat flour

2¼ tsp. baking powder

1 tbsp. sugar or Splenda®

¾ tsp. salt

3 eggs

1½ cups milk

⅓ cup canola oil

1 cup mashed bananas

Sift together all dry ingredients 3 times. Beat eggs, and add milk, oil, and bananas. Stir liquids into dry ingredients and beat until no lumps remain. Bake in greased, preheated waffle iron according to manufacturer's directions until golden brown. Serve hot with Canola Butter (see index) and sugar-free syrup. Yield: 6 servings.

Nutrition Facts

Amount Per Serving

Calories 286 (52% from Fat, 12% from Protein, 36% from Carb)

Total Fat 17 g

  Saturated Fat 2 g

  Mono Fat 9 g

Cholesterol 125 mg

Sodium 538 mg

Total Carbohydrate 26 g

  Dietary Fiber 3 g

  Sugars 9 g

Protein 9 g

Calcium 176 mg

Iron 2 mg

Cinnamon Coffeecake

COFFEECAKE:

1 cup white flour

1 cup white whole-wheat flour

2½ tsp. baking powder

¾ tsp. salt

⅔ cup sugar

2 eggs

1 cup milk

4 tbsp. trans-fat-free shortening

TOPPING:

¼ cup sugar

1 tsp. cinnamon

1 tbsp. white flour

¼ cup melted butter

In large mixing bowl, add all dry cake ingredients and mix. Add wet cake ingredients and beat until smooth. Spread into a greased 8- or 9-in. square pan.

Mix dry topping ingredients and sprinkle on batter. Drizzle with butter. Bake 35-40 min. at 350 degrees, or until toothpick inserted in center comes out clean. Cut into squares and serve warm with Canola Butter (see index). Yield: 9 servings.

Note: This cake also works well using 1 cup white flour, ½ cup white whole-wheat flour, and ½ cup oat flour.

Nutrition Facts	
Amount Per Serving	
Calories 302 (38% from Fat, 7% from Protein, 55% from Carb)	
Total Fat 13 g	
Saturated Fat 5 g	
Mono Fat 5 g	
Cholesterol 69 mg	
Sodium 393 mg	
Total Carbohydrate 43 g	
Dietary Fiber 2 g	
Sugars 21 g	
Protein 5 g	
Calcium 109 mg	
Iron 2 mg	

Almond Coffeecake

COFFEECAKE:

1 egg

½ cup milk

½ cup white flour

½ cup white whole-wheat flour

½ cup sugar

1 tbsp. baking powder

½ tsp. salt

4 tbsp. butter, melted

TOPPING:

2 tbsp. sugar

½ tsp. cinnamon

¼ cup sliced almonds

With electric mixer, beat egg and milk until very fluffy. Sift together flours, sugar, baking powder, and salt twice. Fold into egg and milk mixture. Add butter. Pour into a greased 8-in. square pan.

Mix topping ingredients together, and sprinkle on batter. Bake approximately 15-20 min. in preheated 375-degree oven, or until toothpick inserted in center comes out clean. Cut into squares and serve warm. Yield: 9 servings.

Nutrition Facts
Amount Per Serving
Calories 185 (38% from Fat, 8% from Protein, 54% from Carb)
Total Fat 8 g
Saturated Fat 4 g
Mono Fat 3 g
Cholesterol 41 mg
Sodium 345 mg
Total Carbohydrate 26 g
Dietary Fiber 1 g
Sugars 15 g
Protein 4 g
Calcium 119 mg
Iron 1 mg

Apple Skillet Cake

1½ cups whole-wheat pastry flour

1 tsp. baking soda

1 tsp. salt

1 cup sugar

1 tsp. cinnamon

¾ cup canola oil

½ cup buttermilk

1 egg

2 apples, peeled and sliced

1 tsp. vanilla extract

1 cup pecans, chopped

Sift together dry ingredients. Add remaining ingredients and mix well. Pour batter into lightly greased 9- or 10-in. iron skillet. Bake 40-50 min. in a preheated 350-degree oven.

Cut into wedges. Serve warm with butter or whipped cream. Yield: 10 servings.

Nutrition Facts
Amount Per Serving
Calories 409 (54% from Fat, 4% from Protein, 42% from Carb)
Total Fat 25 g
Saturated Fat 2 g
Mono Fat 14 g
Cholesterol 25 mg
Sodium 377 mg
Total Carbohydrate 45 g
Dietary Fiber 5 g
Sugars 24 g
Protein 5 g
Calcium 31 mg
Iron 2 mg

Blueberry Teacake

TEACAKE:

2 cups whole-wheat pastry flour

½ cup sugar

2 tsp. baking powder

1 tsp. salt

⅔ cup canola oil

1 cup milk

2 eggs

TOPPING:

3 cups blueberries

¼ cup Splenda®

¼ cup sugar

1 tsp. cinnamon

Mix cake ingredients together in a bowl. Pour into a greased 9x13-in. pan.

Mix topping ingredients together. Place on top of cake. Bake 30-40 min. at 350 degrees.

Dust with powdered sugar if desired. Cut into squares and serve warm. Yield: 16 servings.

Nutrition Facts		
Amount Per Serving		
Calories 221 (41% from Fat, 6% from Protein, 53% from Carb)		
Total Fat 10 g		
Saturated Fat 1 g		
Mono Fat 6 g		
Cholesterol 31 mg		
Sodium 224 mg		
Total Carbohydrate 30 g		
Dietary Fiber 3 g		
Sugars 13 g		
Protein 4 g		
Calcium 59 mg		
Iron 1 mg		

Biscuit Mix

1 cup white flour
1 cup white whole-wheat or whole-wheat flour
¼ cup trans-fat-free shortening
1 tsp. salt
2 tbsp. baking powder

Add all ingredients to medium mixing bowl, and beat with electric mixer on low setting until mixture is the consistency of packaged biscuit mix. Do not overmix. You may add ⅔ cup milk to make biscuits. Roll out to ½-in. thickness and cut with 2-in. floured biscuit cutter. Avoid twisting cutter.

Place biscuits on ungreased baking sheet. Bake 8-10 min. in a preheated 450-degree oven. Yield: 12-14 servings.

Note: This mix can be used in any recipe calling for packaged biscuit mix.

Nutrition Facts

Amount Per Serving

Calories 95 (36% from Fat, 9% from Protein, 55% from Carb)

Total Fat 4 g	
Saturated Fat 1 g	
Mono Fat 2 g	
Cholesterol 0 mg	
Sodium 378 mg	
Total Carbohydrate 14 g	
Dietary Fiber	
Sugars 0 g	
Protein 2 g	
Calcium 120 mg	
Iron 1 mg	

Cheddar Biscuits

2 cups Biscuit Mix (see previous recipe)
⅔ cup milk
½ cup regular or low-fat shredded cheddar cheese
¼ cup butter or Canola Butter (see index), melted
¼ tsp. garlic powder

Combine Biscuit Mix, milk, and cheese. Beat with a wooden spoon for about 30 seconds.

Drop onto an ungreased baking sheet. Smooth the tops down with a spoon. Bake 8-10 min. at 450 degrees.

Combine butter and garlic powder and pour over hot biscuits. Yield: 12-14 servings.

Nutrition Facts

Amount Per Serving

Calories 147 (54% from Fat, 9% from Protein, 37% from Carb)

Total Fat 9 g

  Saturated Fat 4 g

  Mono Fat 3 g

Cholesterol 14 mg

Sodium 433 mg

Total Carbohydrate 14 g

  Dietary Fiber 1 g

  Sugars 0 g

Protein 4 g

Calcium 162 mg

Iron 1 mg

Buttermilk Biscuits

1 cup white flour
1 cup white whole-wheat flour
2 tsp. baking powder
¼ tsp. baking soda
½ cup trans-fat-free butter shortening
1 cup buttermilk
Melted butter

Sift dry ingredients together and cut in shortening with 2 crisscrossed knives or pastry blender. Add buttermilk and stir until a dough is formed. Knead several times on floured board.

Roll out to ½-in. thickness and cut with 2-in. floured biscuit cutter or glass. Avoid twisting cutter. Brush tops with butter.

Place biscuits close together on an ungreased baking sheet and bake until golden brown, approximately 8-10 min., in a preheated 450-degree oven.

To make cheddar biscuits from this recipe, remove biscuits from oven a few minutes before done and sprinkle shredded cheese on top. Return to oven just until cheese has melted. Yield: 12-14 servings.

Nutrition Facts

Amount Per Serving

Calories 130 (52% from Fat, 7% from Protein, 41% from Carb)

Total Fat 8 g

  Saturated Fat 2 g

  Mono Fat 3 g

Cholesterol 0 mg

Sodium 102 mg

Total Carbohydrate 14 g

  Dietary Fiber 1 g

  Sugars 0 g

Protein 2 g

Calcium 53 mg

Iron 1 mg

Yogurt Biscuits

1 cup white flour
1 cup white whole-wheat flour
1 tbsp. baking powder
¼ tsp. baking soda
1 tsp. salt
1 cup plain yogurt
¼ cup canola oil

Sift together dry ingredients. Make a well in center and add yogurt and oil. Mix just until combined.

Place on floured board, knead a few times, and roll out with rolling pin to ½-in. thickness. Use 2-in. biscuit cutter dipped in flour to cut out 12 rounds. Avoid twisting cutter.

Place biscuits on an ungreased baking sheet. Bake 10-12 min. in a preheated 375-degree oven, or until lightly browned. Yield: 12 servings.

Nutrition Facts

Amount Per Serving

Calories 125 (36% from Fat, 11% from Protein, 53% from Carb)

Total Fat 5 g	
Saturated Fat 1 g	
Mono Fat 3 g	
Cholesterol 1 mg	
Sodium 360 mg	
Total Carbohydrate 17g	
Dietary Fiber 2 g	
Sugars 2 g	
Protein 4 g	
Calcium 110 mg	
Iron 1 mg	

Coconut Scones

1¾ cups whole-wheat pastry flour
½ cup sweetened flaked coconut
½ cup rolled oats
3 tbsp. sugar or Splenda®
2 tsp. baking powder
¼ tsp. salt
⅓ cup cold butter, sliced
2 eggs
½ cup milk
¼ cup sugar-free or reduced-sugar jam or preserves

In large bowl, combine flour, coconut, oats, 2 tbsp. sugar or Splenda®, baking powder, and salt. With hands or pastry blender, cut in butter until coarse crumbs are formed.

In small bowl, beat eggs and milk together. Stir all but approximately 1 tbsp. egg mixture into flour mixture just until evenly moistened.

Turn dough onto lightly floured board and pat into an 8-in. round. Slide onto a greased baking sheet and cut into 8 wedges. Leave wedges in place. Brush top of scones with reserved egg mixture and sprinkle with remaining 1 tbsp. sugar.

Make a 1-in.-diameter depression on top of the wide end of each wedge and fill each with approximately ½ tbsp. jam.

Bake 18-20 min. at 375 degrees or until golden brown. Re-cut the scones to separate. Serve warm. Yield: 8 servings.

Nutrition Facts

Amount Per Serving

Calories 287 (36% from Fat, 9% from Protein, 55% from Carb)

Total Fat 12 g	
Saturated Fat 7 g	
Mono Fat 3 g	
Cholesterol 82 mg	
Sodium 300 mg	
Total Carbohydrate 42 g	
Dietary Fiber 5 g	
Sugars 11 g	
Protein 7 g	
Calcium 106 mg	
Iron 3 mg	

Raisin-Oatmeal Scones

¾ cup whole-wheat flour
¾ cup white flour
1 cup rolled oats
1 tsp. baking soda
½ tsp. salt
¼ cup canola oil
½ cup raisins
¾ cup sour milk* or buttermilk
Canola Butter (see index)

Mix dry ingredients. Combine oil, raisins, and milk. Quickly stir into dry ingredients, combining just until mixed. Flour hands and place dough on a greased baking sheet.

Pat into circle about ½ in. thick. Cut into 6 wedges and separate each wedge. Brush top of each scone with a little oil.

Bake approximately 20 min. at 400 degrees. Serve with butter and, if you desire, sugar-free jam. Yield: 4-6 servings.

Note: I have also made this recipe with 1½ cups pastry flour.

*Milk can be soured by adding 2 tsp. vinegar to ¾ cup milk.

Nutrition Facts

Amount Per Serving

Calories 338 (31% from Fat, 10% from Protein, 59% from Carb)

Total Fat 12 g	
Saturated Fat 1 g	
Mono Fat 6 g	
Cholesterol 1 mg	
Sodium 415 mg	
Total Carbohydrate 52 g	
Dietary Fiber 6 g	
Sugars 9 g	
Protein 9 g	
Calcium 44 mg	
Iron 3 mg	

Strawberry Cream Crêpes

CREPES:

2 eggs
¼ cup whole-wheat flour
¼ cup white flour
1 tbsp. sugar or Splenda®
½ cup milk
2 tbsp. water
1½ tsp. melted butter or canola oil

FILLING:

3 cups fresh strawberries
⅓ cup Splenda®
1 cup cottage cheese
½ cup sour cream
½ cup plain yogurt
½ cup Splenda®

For crêpes, beat eggs in mixing bowl. Gradually add flours and sugar or Splenda® alternately with milk and water, beating with whisk until smooth. Beat in butter. Refrigerate batter for at least 1 hour.

For filling, slice strawberries, add ⅓ cup Splenda®, and set aside. In blender, whip cottage cheese until smooth. Stir in sour cream, yogurt, and ½ cup Splenda®.

Brush a small skillet or crêpe pan with oil, and heat pan on stove on medium high. When hot, add 2-3 tbsp. batter while lifting pan above heat. Immediately tilt pan in all directions, swirling batter so it spreads over bottom of pan. Return to heat and cook until bottom of crêpe is browned. Turn with spatula and brown other side for a few seconds. Remove from pan and repeat process, stacking each crêpe on a plate when done.

Nutrition Facts		
Amount Per Serving		
Calories 100 (36% from Fat, 20% from Protein, 44% from Carb)		
Total Fat 4 g		
Saturated Fat 2 g		
Mono Fat 1 g		
Cholesterol 48 mg		
Sodium 33 mg		
Total Carbohydrate 11 g		
Dietary Fiber 1 g		
Sugars 4 g		
Protein 5 g		
Calcium 52 mg		
Iron 1 mg		

Fill each crêpe with "cream" and strawberries. Fold like an upside-down enchilada, reserving some of the filling and berries to garnish top of each crêpe. Yield: 12 servings.

Plain Muffins

1 cup white flour
1 cup white whole-wheat flour
½ tsp. salt
1 tbsp. baking powder
2 tbsp. sugar
1 egg
1¼ cups milk
3 tbsp. melted butter or canola oil

Sift together dry ingredients. In separate bowl, beat egg. Add milk and butter or canola oil to egg and blend. Make a well in center of dry ingredients and pour wet ingredients into well. Stir quickly until combined but do not overmix. Batter will be lumpy.

Fill greased muffin-tin cavities ⅔ full. Bake 20 min. in a preheated 425-degree oven, or until golden brown. Remove muffins immediately from tin. Serve hot with Canola Butter (see index). Yield: 12 servings.

VARIATIONS:

Cinnamon Apple Muffins: Add 1 cup applesauce or sliced apples and ½ tsp. cinnamon to batter before baking.

Berry Muffins: Add 1 cup berries to batter before baking.

Nut Muffins: Add ½ cup chopped nuts to batter before baking.

Nutrition Facts
Amount Per Serving
Calories 121 (30% from Fat, 11% from Protein, 59% from Carb)
Total Fat 4 g
Saturated Fat 2 g
Mono Fat 1 g
Cholesterol 29 mg
Sodium 253 mg
Total Carbohydrate 18 g
Dietary Fiber 2 g
Sugars 3 g
Protein 4 g
Calcium 91 mg
Iron 1 mg

Chocolate Chunk Muffins

6 tbsp. butter or Canola Butter (see index)
4 oz. bittersweet chocolate, coarsely chopped
1 cup white flour
1 cup white whole-wheat flour
¼ cup sugar
⅓ cup unsweetened cocoa powder
1 tbsp. baking powder
½ tsp. baking soda
½ tsp. salt
1¼ cups buttermilk
1 egg
1 tsp. vanilla extract

In microwave, melt together butter and half of the chopped chocolate.

In large bowl, sift together flours, sugar, cocoa, baking powder, baking soda, and salt.

In smaller bowl, whisk together buttermilk, egg, and vanilla until well combined.

Pour milk and chocolate mixtures over dry ingredients. Gently but quickly stir to combine. Do not overmix. Stir in remaining chopped chocolate.

Divide batter among 12 greased muffin-tin cavities. Bake approximately 20 min. in a preheated 375-degree oven. Cool 5 min. before removing from pan. Yield: 12 servings.

Nutrition Facts

Amount Per Serving

Calories 206 (47% from Fat, 9% from Protein, 43% from Carb)

Total Fat 12 g	
Saturated Fat 7 g	
Mono Fat 3 g	
Cholesterol 36 mg	
Sodium 338 mg	
Total Carbohydrate 25 g	
Dietary Fiber 4 g	
Sugars 5 g	
Protein 5 g	
Calcium 105 mg	
Iron 3 mg	

Two-Ingredient Muffins

1 (18.25-oz.) pkg. chocolate cake mix, regular or reduced sugar
1 (15-oz.) can pumpkin puree

Mix together and fill greased muffin-tin cavities ⅔ full. Bake approximately 20-25 min. at 350 degrees, until toothpick inserted in center comes out clean. Remove muffins immediately from tin and serve hot. Extra muffins can be frozen. Yield: 18 servings.

Note: Be sure to buy pumpkin puree and not pumpkin-pie filling.

Nutrition Facts
Amount Per Serving
Calories 27 (18% from Fat, 4% from Protein, 79% from Carb)
Total Fat 1 g
Saturated Fat 0 g
Mono Fat 0 g
Cholesterol 0 mg
Sodium 45 mg
Total Carbohydrate 5 g
Dietary Fiber 0 g
Sugars 3 g
Protein 0 g
Calcium 11 mg
Iron 0 mg

Graham Muffins

1 cup white flour
1 cup graham or whole-wheat flour
¼ tsp. salt
4 tbsp. baking powder
¼ cup honey or brown sugar
2 eggs, well beaten
3 tbsp. canola oil
1 cup milk
½ cup raisins, optional

In medium mixing bowl, sift together flours, salt, and baking powder.

In separate bowl, blend together remaining ingredients.

Make a well in center of dry ingredients and add wet ingredients. Stir until just blended, being careful not to overmix. Add to greased muffin-tin cavities, filling each ⅔ full.

Bake 15-20 min. at 375 degrees. Remove muffins immediately from tin. Serve hot with Canola Butter (see index). Yield: 12 servings.

Nutrition Facts		
Amount Per Serving		
Calories 167 (26% from Fat, 10% from Protein, 65% from Carb)		
Total Fat 5 g		
Saturated Fat 1 g		
Mono Fat 2 g		
Cholesterol 42 mg		
Sodium 556 mg		
Total Carbohydrate 28 g		
Dietary Fiber 2 g		
Sugars 11 g		
Protein 4 g		
Calcium 296 mg		
Iron 2 mg		

Bran Muffins

1¼ cups whole-wheat flour
⅓ cup brown sugar
½ tsp. salt
2½ tsp. baking powder
¾-1 cup bran
½ cup walnuts, chopped
1 egg, beaten
¾ cup milk
¼ cup canola oil
1 cup unsweetened applesauce
½ cup raisins

Stir together flour, sugar, salt, baking powder, bran, and walnuts. In separate bowl, combine remaining ingredients. Make a well in center of dry ingredients, and add wet ingredients all at once. Stir only until moistened. Do not overmix.

Fill 12 greased muffin cups each ⅔ full. Bake approximately 20 min. at 400 degrees, or until lightly browned and toothpick inserted in center comes out clean. Remove muffins immediately from muffin cups. Serve hot with Canola Butter (see index). Yield: 12 servings.

Nutrition Facts		
Amount Per Serving		
Calories 189 (38% from Fat, 9% from Protein, 52% from Carb)		
Total Fat 9 g		
Saturated Fat 1 g		
Mono Fat 4 g		
Cholesterol 21 mg		
Sodium 214 mg		
Total Carbohydrate 27 g		
Dietary Fiber 4 g		
Sugars 13 g		
Protein 5 g		
Calcium 87 mg		
Iron 2 mg		

Dark Bran Muffins

1 cup white whole-wheat or whole-wheat flour
2 cups wheat bran
1 cup oat bran
2 tsp. baking soda
1 tsp. baking powder
½ tsp. salt
2 eggs
⅔ cup milk
⅔ cup plain yogurt
⅓ cup canola oil
½ cup molasses
1 tsp. vanilla extract
1 cup raisins

In large bowl, mix together flour, brans, baking soda, baking powder, and salt. In separate bowl, blend together wet ingredients, and then add raisins. Make a well in center of dry ingredients, and add wet ingredients. Quickly stir just until combined.

Fill greased muffin-tin cavities about ⅔ full. Bake 20-25 min. in a preheated 375-degree oven. Remove muffins immediately from tin. Serve hot with Canola Butter (see index). Yield: 12-14 servings.

Nutrition Facts

Amount Per Serving

Calories 199 (29% from Fat, 9% from Protein, 61% from Carb)

Total Fat 7 g	
Saturated Fat 1 g	
Mono Fat 4 g	
Cholesterol 36 mg	
Sodium 339 mg	
Total Carbohydrate 34 g	
Dietary Fiber 5 g	
Sugars 15 g	
Protein 5 g	
Calcium 97 mg	
Iron 3 mg	

Amish Raisin Bran Muffins

2½ cups whole-wheat flour

1 cup soy flour

1½ cups white flour

1 (10-oz.) box raisin bran flakes

2 tbsp. baking soda

1 cup sugar

1 tbsp. salt

4 cups buttermilk

4 eggs, beaten

1 cup canola oil

Mix together all dry ingredients. Add wet ingredients and mix quickly. Do not overmix. Dough will keep in refrigerator for 6 weeks.

Bake all at 1 time if preferred, approximately 12-15 min. in greased muffin tin at 400 degrees, or until done. Remove muffins immediately from tin. Serve hot with Canola Butter (see index). Extra muffins can be frozen. Yield: 36 servings.

Note: King Arthur® white whole-wheat flour has all of the fiber and nutrition of traditional whole-wheat flour. If you prefer not to mix your own flours, this is a good substitute for the 3 flours used in this recipe.

Nutrition Facts

Amount Per Serving

Calories 174 (39% from Fat, 10% from Protein, 51% from Carb)

Total Fat 8 g

  Saturated Fat 1 g

  Mono Fat 4 g

Cholesterol 28 mg

Sodium 462 mg

Total Carbohydrate 23 g

  Dietary Fiber 2 g

  Sugars 9 g

Protein 4 g

Calcium 175 mg

Iron 3 mg

Gingerbread-Jam Muffins

MUFFINS:

1 cup unsweetened applesauce

¼ cup canola oil

¼ cup firmly packed brown sugar

1 large egg, lightly beaten

1 cup white whole-wheat flour

1 cup all-purpose flour

2 tsp. baking powder

½ tsp. salt

1 tsp. ginger

1½ tsp. cinnamon

⅛ tsp. ground cloves

⅓ cup sugar-free raspberry jam

TOPPING:

½ tsp. cinnamon

2 tbsp. sugar or Splenda®

For muffins, in large bowl, blend together applesauce, oil, sugar, and egg. Into this mixture, sift flours, baking powder, salt, ginger, cinnamon, and cloves; beat until just combined.

Spoon batter into greased muffin tin, filling each cup halfway. Spoon 1 tsp. jam on top of each muffin, and top with remaining batter.

For topping, in small bowl, combine cinnamon and sugar. Sprinkle ½ tsp. cinnamon sugar on top of each muffin. Bake 35 min. at 350 degrees, or until golden brown. Let cool in pan 5 minutes, and serve warm. Yield: 12 servings.

Nutrition Facts	
Amount Per Serving	
Calories 165 (28% from Fat, 7% from Protein, 65% from Carb)	
Total Fat 5 g	
Saturated Fat 1 g	
Mono Fat 3 g	
Cholesterol 20 mg	
Sodium 190 mg	
Total Carbohydrate 29 g	
Dietary Fiber 3 g	
Sugars 9 g	
Protein 3 g	
Calcium 72 mg	
Iron 2 mg	

Oatmeal Muffins

1 cup buttermilk
1 egg
½ cup canola oil
1 cup rolled oats
½ cup soy flour
½ cup whole-wheat flour
1 tsp. baking powder
1 tsp. baking soda
½ tsp. salt
½ tsp. cinnamon
¼ cup brown sugar
½ cup raisins, optional

In small bowl, combine milk, egg, and oil. In separate larger bowl, combine rest of ingredients. Make a well in center of dry ingredients, and add wet ingredients. Stir or whisk together quickly just until combined. Do not overmix.

Spoon batter into greased muffin tin. Bake 15-20 min. at 400 degrees, or until done. Remove muffins immediately from tin. Serve hot with Canola Butter (see index). Yield: 12 servings.

Note: Traditional recipes call for white flour, vegetable oil, ½ cup brown sugar, and 1 cup raisins.

Nutrition Facts

Amount Per Serving

Calories 214 (47% from Fat, 10% from Protein, 44% from Carb)

Total Fat 12 g	
Saturated Fat 1 g	
Mono Fat 6 g	
Cholesterol 21 mg	
Sodium 263 mg	
Total Carbohydrate 24 g	
Dietary Fiber 3 g	
Sugars 9 g	
Protein 5 g	
Calcium 64 mg	
Iron 1 mg	

Snickerdoodle Muffins

MUFFINS:

1 cup Canola Butter (see index) or Smart Balance® regular spread

¼ cup sugar

2 tsp. vanilla extract

2 eggs

1¼ cups white flour

1 cup white whole-wheat flour

¾ tsp. baking soda

¾ tsp. baking powder

¾ tsp. cream of tartar

¾ tsp. nutmeg

1¼ cups regular or light sour cream

TOPPING:

¼ cup sugar

¼ cup Splenda®

2 tbsp. cinnamon

With electric mixer, cream together butter and sugar for 4 min. Add vanilla. Add eggs 1 at a time until blended.

In separate bowl, combine dry ingredients.

Add flour mixture and sour cream alternately to butter mixture in several additions, starting and ending with flour. Scrape bowl occasionally.

Mix together topping ingredients.

Fill greased muffin tins ⅔ full and sprinkle each with topping. Bake approximately 12-14 min. in a preheated 350-degree oven, or until toothpick inserted in center comes out clean. Remove muffins immediately from tins, and serve hot with Canola Butter. Yield: 12-14 servings.

Nutrition Facts
Amount Per Serving
Calories 284 (60% from Fat, 6% from Protein, 34% from Carb)
Total Fat 19 g
Saturated Fat 9 g
Mono Fat 7 g
Cholesterol 67 mg
Sodium 179 mg
Total Carbohydrate 24 g
Dietary Fiber 2 g
Sugars 7 g
Protein 4 g
Calcium 62 mg
Iron 1 mg

Mandarin Orange Muffins

MUFFINS:

1 (11-oz.) can mandarin oranges

¾ cup white flour

¾ cup white whole-wheat flour

1¾ tsp. baking powder

½ tsp. salt

¼ tsp. nutmeg

¼ tsp. allspice

⅓ cup sugar

⅓ cup Canola Butter (see index) or Smart Balance® regular spread

1 egg, lightly beaten

⅓ cup milk

TOPPING:

¼ cup Splenda®

½ tsp. cinnamon

¼ cup melted Canola Butter (see index) or Smart Balance® regular spread

For muffins, drain mandarin oranges and pat dry with a paper towel; set aside.

Combine dry ingredients and cut in butter or spread. Add oranges and mix lightly.

In separate bowl, combine egg and milk. Add all at once to flour mixture and mix just until combined.

Fill greased muffin tin with batter until ¾ full. Bake 20-25 min. in a preheated 350-degree oven.

For topping, combine Splenda® and cinnamon. Remove muffins from tin, dip tops of muffins in butter or spread, and then roll tops in cinnamon mixture. Serve hot with Canola Butter. Yield: 12 servings.

Nutrition Facts	
Amount Per Serving	
Calories 184 (51% from Fat, 6% from Protein, 43% from Carb)	
Total Fat 11 g	
Saturated Fat 3 g	
Mono Fat 5 g	
Cholesterol 33 mg	
Sodium 211 mg	
Total Carbohydrate 20 g	
Dietary Fiber 2 g	
Sugars 8 g	
Protein 3 g	
Calcium 56 mg	
Iron 1 mg	

Lemon Poppyseed Muffins

2 eggs

1 cup milk

1 tbsp. lemon juice

2 tbsp. lemon zest

¼ cup canola oil

1 cup white flour

1 cup white whole-wheat flour

¼ cup sugar

2½ tsp. baking powder

¼ tsp. nutmeg

2 tbsp. poppyseeds

½ cup walnuts, chopped

In large bowl, by hand, beat together eggs, milk, lemon juice, lemon zest, and oil until blended. Combine dry ingredients. Add to wet ingredients and stir just until combined.

Fill greased muffin tins ¾ full. Bake approximately 20 min. in a preheated 400-degree oven, or until toothpick inserted in center comes out clean. Remove muffins immediately from tins. Serve hot. Yield: 12 servings.

Nutrition Facts

Amount Per Serving

Calories 190 (45% from Fat, 11% from Protein, 44% from Carb)

Total Fat 10 g	
Saturated Fat 1 g	
Mono Fat 4 g	
Cholesterol 42 mg	
Sodium 120 mg	
Total Carbohydrate 21 g	
Dietary Fiber 2 g	
Sugars 5 g	
Protein 6 g	
Calcium 104 mg	
Iron 1 mg	

Corn Muffins

1 cup white whole-wheat flour
¾ cup yellow cornmeal
3 tbsp. sugar
2 tsp. baking powder
1 tsp. salt
1 egg
1 cup milk
¼ cup canola oil

In large bowl, combine dry ingredients. In smaller bowl, combine wet ingredients. Make a well in center of dry ingredients and add wet ingredients. Stir just until moistened.

Fill greased muffin-tin cavities ⅔ full. Bake 16-18 min. in a preheated 400-degree oven, or until toothpick inserted in center comes out clean. Remove muffins immediately from tin. Yield: 8 servings.

Note: I sometimes make this recipe with ½ cup white flour and ½ cup white whole-wheat flour.

Nutrition Facts

Amount Per Serving

Calories 197 (38% from Fat, 9% from Protein, 53% from Carb)

Total Fat 9 g

Saturated Fat 1 g

Mono Fat 5 g

Cholesterol 32 mg

Sodium 434 mg

Total Carbohydrate 27 g

Dietary Fiber 3 g

Sugars 6 g

Protein 5 g

Calcium 95 mg

Iron 1 mg

Buttermilk Cornbread

4 tbsp. butter
¼ cup canola oil
¼ cup sugar
2 eggs
1 cup buttermilk
½ tsp. baking soda
1 cup cornmeal
⅓ cup all-purpose flour
⅓ cup soy flour
⅓ cup whole-wheat flour
½ tsp. salt

Melt butter and pour into large mixing bowl. Add oil, and stir in sugar. Add eggs and beat until well blended. Combine buttermilk with baking soda and add to bowl. Stir in cornmeal, flours, and salt until well blended. Pour batter into a greased 8-in. square pan.

Bake 30-40 min. in a preheated 375-degree oven, or until toothpick inserted in center comes out clean. Yield: 9 servings.

Note: This cornbread does not rise or brown much. It is moist and very tasty!

Nutrition Facts		
Amount Per Serving		
Calories 249 (49% from Fat, 9% from Protein, 42% from Carb)		
Total Fat 14 g		
Saturated Fat 4 g		
Mono Fat 6 g		
Cholesterol 69 mg		
Sodium 268 mg		
Total Carbohydrate 26 g		
Dietary Fiber 2 g		
Sugars 7 g		
Protein 6 g		
Calcium 37 mg		
Iron 1 mg		

Chapter 6

Sourdough and Starters

For those who miss white bread and white flour products, recent studies show that sourdough bread products can actually be more effective than whole-wheat breads in minimizing spikes in blood sugar. It is thought that the lactic acid produced during the fermentation of the sourdough changes the nature of the starches in the bread, making it more beneficial for blood glucose levels.

Sourdough bread is leavened by capturing wild yeasts in a dough or batter. It has a distinct tangy or sour taste that comes from the normal aging process. Sourdough is made from a starter dough, which contains the yeast culture. A small amount (20 to 25 percent) of this starter dough is mixed with new flour and water. Part of this resulting dough is then saved to use as the starter for the next batch. Each time you use 1 cup starter, you should replace that with 1 cup of your new starter, for next time.

There are many variations for sourdough starter. It can be made with water, milk or buttermilk, wheat flour, whole-wheat flour, bread flour, or rye flour. Fruit juice can be added, as can yeast, yogurt, or potato water. There are even more variations than these!

Sourdough will add a new dimension to your baking. My husband and I were blown away by the unique smell and taste sensations we experienced with sourdough baking. The first sourdough recipe I ever attempted was a waffle. It was crisper than any waffle I had ever eaten, and it had the pleasant aromas of both yeast and beer. The taste reminded me a bit of a sourdough pretzel. I then completely understood the appeal of sourdough, and I've been baking with it ever since.

Sourdough baking is typically a 3-step process. The first step involves making your starter. As long as you keep your starter alive, you will not have to repeat this step. Step 2 is typically done the evening before you begin your baking. This is when you make your Basic Sourdough Batter and is also referred to as feeding or refreshing your starter. This batter is used as the basis of virtually all sourdough recipes. You can omit this step if you are just beginning your starter. In that case, you can use half of your starter the next morning as your Basic Sourdough Batter. Step 3 involves using your Basic Sourdough Batter in your chosen recipe.

You can use just about any sourdough starter recipe in any sourdough recipe you come across. I am including several sourdough starter recipes in this chapter. But first, here are a few tips.

- Before going full force into this realm of baking, I recommend testing your blood sugar after consuming sourdough products to see how you respond to them.

- Never use any sort of metal bowl, utensil, or container when working with sourdough, as metal reacts with sourdough. I typically use a ceramic or glass bowl, wooden spoon or silicone or plastic spatula for mixing, and lidded glass or plastic container for refrigerated storage.

- For best results, always use unbleached flour when making your starter.

- Exact measurements of flour are difficult to give with sourdough, as each starter is different. You'll have to use your own judgment at times.

- It is recommended that you not use chlorinated tap water when making your starter, as it can stop the sourdough from rising.

- Sourdough starter can be purchased in a dried state for mixing, if you prefer not to make your own.

- Many people find yeast-based starters to be more foolproof. Purists prefer a starter made of flour and water only.

- As your starter matures, it should smell like yeast or beer.

- Your starter will get better with age.

- If a starter is not to be used for several weeks, it can be frozen or dried.

- Heat over 95 degrees will kill the yeast or starter.

- If your starter becomes too sour, you can add a pinch of baking soda to sweeten it.

- If the liquid in the refrigerated starter begins to separate, stir it or sweeten it with 1 tsp. sugar. The liquid can also be poured off. This liquid is often referred to as "the hooch."

- Most sourdough starters are unsuitable for use in bread machines.

- Your sourdough starter is a living, breathing thing, so it must be fed with flour and water or it will die. Feed it every 7-10 days or so and it should live happily ever after!

- Cleanliness is very important when creating and working with your sourdough starter. You don't want to pick up any harmful bacteria, which can ruin your results.

- When refreshing the Basic Sourdough Batter, you may add other types of flour than the one you originally used.

- Sourdough breads typically take longer to rise, and a second rise is not always necessary.

- Whole-wheat flour typically does not rise as well as white or bread flour in sourdough recipes.

- If your starter turns pink or orange, grows mold, or smells off, discard it and start over.

- Remember to always make extra Basic Sourdough Batter so you have starter to put in your refrigerator for future baking.

Sourdough Starter I

1 cup unbleached flour
1 cup warm water, filtered or bottled

Blend together and pour into a wide-mouthed glass jar. Cover and keep in a warm place, but note that temperatures over 95 degrees will kill the yeast.

Every 24 hours, throw out half (you can use this in non-yeasted recipes such as pancakes, waffles, tea breads, or cakes). Add ½ cup flour and ½ cup water. Within 3-4 days (sometimes sooner and sometimes later), you should notice lots of bubbles and a pleasant sour or beer smell. At this point, you will refrigerate the sourdough starter with a loose-fitting lid.

Sourdough Starter II

2 cups unbleached flour
2 cups warm water, filtered or bottled
1 pkg. dry yeast

In bowl, mix together all ingredients. Keep in a warm place overnight, such as inside an oven with the light lit. The next morning, the mixture should be bubbly. Remove 1 cup starter mixture, put this in a covered container, and store in refrigerator for future use. Replenish every week with flour and water, and the starter will last for years. The remaining 1 cup starter mixture can be used immediately in your desired recipe.

Basic Sourdough Batter

1 cup sourdough starter
2 cups warm water, filtered or bottled
2 cups flour (white, whole wheat, rye, etc.)

This is what you use when a recipe calls for sourdough starter. Basic Sourdough Batter should always be used at room temperature.

Place sourdough starter in a large bowl that allows for expansion. Add water and flour and stir until thoroughly mixed. The mixture will be thick and lumpy. Cover and put in warm place overnight. In the morning, batter will be thin and fermented with bubbles.

Conversion Basic Sourdough Batter

1 cup sourdough starter
Approximately ⅔ of the flour called for in the recipe
All of the milk or water in the recipe

You can convert your existing yeasted recipes to sourdough versions by making this Conversion Basic Sourdough Batter.

Combine all ingredients above in large bowl. This should make a thick batter, not a dough. Cover bowl and set in warm place for 14-16 hours. Mixture will be bubbly and light. This ensures your recipe will rise.

Add all of ingredients the recipe calls for except remaining flour. *Do not add any yeast, baking powder, or baking soda.*

Add remaining flour and knead by hand. Only add more flour if needed to make a soft, non-sticky, pliable dough. Dough should be smooth and elastic but a bit softer than a typical yeast dough.

Let dough rise 10 min., covered.

Form dough into loaf or rolls as recipe specifies.

In a warm spot, let dough rise to top of pan or until light and puffy. Dough will take much longer to rise than normal. Be patient!

Bake according to recipe directions.

Sourdough Pancakes

1 cup flour of your choice

¾ tsp. baking soda

1 tsp. baking powder

½ tsp. salt

2 tbsp. sugar or Splenda®

½ cup oat bran, wheat bran, or wheat germ, optional

1 cup sourdough starter

⅓ cup canola oil

2 eggs

½ cup milk

1 tsp. vanilla extract

In large mixing bowl, combine dry ingredients. In separate smaller bowl, combine wet ingredients, including starter.

Add wet ingredients to dry ingredients and mix well. Drop by ¼ cupfuls onto lightly greased griddle. Cook until bubbles form and edges start to dry. Turn and cook other side. Yield: 24 servings.

Nutrition Facts

Amount Per Serving

Calories 81 (43% from Fat, 9% from Protein, 49% from Carb)

Total Fat 4 g	
Saturated Fat 0 g	
Mono Fat 2 g	
Cholesterol 21 mg	
Sodium 117 mg	
Total Carbohydrate 10 g	
Dietary Fiber 0 g	
Sugars 1 g	
Protein 2 g	
Calcium 19 mg	
Iron 1 mg	

Sourdough Waffles

1 egg
4 tbsp. canola oil
¼ cup milk
4 cups Basic Sourdough Batter
1 tsp. salt
1 tsp. baking soda

Add egg, oil, and milk to batter. Mix together salt and baking soda, and sprinkle over batter. Mix together gently. Let rest 5 min. More milk can be added if mixture is too thick.

Pour into very hot greased waffle iron and cook according to manufacturer's directions. Yield: 6 servings.

Nutrition Facts	
Amount Per Serving	
Calories 300 (33% from Fat, 10% from Protein, 58% from Carb)	
Total Fat 11 g	
Saturated Fat 1 g	
Mono Fat 6 g	
Cholesterol 41 mg	
Sodium 619 mg	
Total Carbohydrate 43 g	
Dietary Fiber 2 g	
Sugars 0 g	
Protein 7 g	
Calcium 19 mg	
Iron 3 mg	

Sourdough Biscuits I

1 cup Basic Sourdough Batter
Favorite biscuit recipe minus ½ cup flour and ½ cup liquid

Add batter to biscuit ingredients, minus ½ cup flour and ½ cup liquid. Proceed according to recipe directions.

Sourdough Biscuits II

2 cups flour
1 tbsp. baking powder
1 tsp. salt
1 tbsp. sugar
3 tbsp. butter, melted and cooled
2 cups sourdough starter
Additional melted butter

Sift together dry ingredients. Add cooled butter and sourdough starter and mix to form firm dough. Knead a few times until smooth. Pinch off dough the size of walnuts and roll into balls, or roll out and cut with biscuit cutter. Place on buttered pan or in muffin tins. Cover and let sit in warm place 15 min. Bake 20-30 min. in a preheated 400-degree oven, until golden brown. Remove from oven and brush with butter. Yield: 24 servings.

Note: For softer rolls, add 2 tsp. dough enhancer (optional), ¼ cup milk, and ¼ cup additional flour. Dough enhancer can be purchased online at: www.beprepared.com.

Nutrition Facts
Amount Per Serving
Calories 85 (17% from Fat, 10% from Protein, 73% from Carb)
Total Fat 2 g
Saturated Fat 1 g
Mono Fat 0 g
Cholesterol 4 mg
Sodium 170 mg
Total Carbohydrate 15 g
Dietary Fiber 1 g
Sugars 1 g
Protein 2 g
Calcium 37 mg
Iron 1 mg

Sourdough Buns

1 pkg. yeast
¼ cup warm water
1 cup sourdough starter
¼ cup butter, melted
½ tsp. salt
1 egg, beaten
2 cups flour

Dissolve yeast in water. Add starter.

Combine butter, salt, and egg. Add sourdough mixture. Stir well, adding flour gradually until a soft dough is formed. A bit of extra flour may be needed.

Place dough in greased bowl, cover, and let rise until double in size. Form into buns. Bake approximately 20-25 min. in a preheated 350-degree oven. Yield: Approximately 16 servings.

Note: You can brush buns with egg white and sprinkle sesame or poppy seeds on top before baking, if desired.

Nutrition Facts

Amount Per Serving

Calories 107 (29% from Fat, 10% from Protein, 61% from Carb)

Total Fat 3 g	
Saturated Fat 2 g	
Mono Fat 1 g	
Cholesterol 23 mg	
Sodium 100 mg	
Total Carbohydrate 16 g	
Dietary Fiber 1 g	
Sugars 0 g	
Protein 3 g	
Calcium 6 mg	
Iron 1 mg	

Soft-Crust Sourdough Bread

½ cup sourdough starter

¾ cup warm water

¾ tsp. salt

⅛ cup sugar

¼ cup canola oil

3 cups bread flour, sifted

In large mixing bowl, combine starter, water, salt, sugar, and oil. Add flour and mix well. Oil dough, place in oiled bowl, and cover. Place in a warm spot and let rise overnight.

The next morning, knead dough for approximately 10 min. Divide in half and place in 2 greased 4x8-in. loaf pans. Allow dough to double in size.

Bake 40-45 min. in a preheated 350-degree oven, or until golden brown and breads sound hollow when tapped. Remove from pans and let cool. Yield: 32 servings.

Nutrition Facts		
Amount Per Serving		
Calories 138 (25% from Fat, 10% from Protein, 65% from Carb)		
Total Fat 4 g		
Saturated Fat 0 g		
Mono Fat 2 g		
Cholesterol 0 mg		
Sodium 111 mg		
Total Carbohydrate 22 g		
Dietary Fiber 1 g		
Sugars 2 g		
Protein 3 g		
Calcium 4 mg		
Iron 1 mg		

Hard-Crust Sourdough Bread

2 eggs
2 pkgs yeast
1¼ cups warm water (105-110 degrees)
1 cup sourdough starter (room temperature)
⅛ cup sugar
¾ tsp. kosher salt
¼ cup canola oil
4-5 cups unbleached flour, divided
Melted butter

Place unbroken eggs in some warm water and let sit 15 min.

Warm the mixing bowl of a stand mixer by filling with hot water, pouring it out, and towel drying bowl.

Add the 1¼ cups warm water to warmed mixing bowl, add yeast, and stir. Let sit 5 min.

On lowest speed of mixer, with dough attachment, stir in starter, sugar, salt, beaten eggs, oil, and 3 cups flour.

Gradually add remaining flour, or enough so dough pulls away from sides of bowl (approximately 8 min.).

Place in oiled bowl, turning to grease all sides. Cover and let rise in a warm place 1-1½ hours, or until double in size.

Punch down, divide dough in half, and shape each half into a loaf. Place loaves in greased 9x5x3-in. loaf pans. Brush tops with oil. Cover loaves and let rise again in a warm place, approximately 1 hour or until double in size.

Bake 30-35 min. in a preheated 375-degree oven, or until breads sound hollow when tapped. Remove from pans and brush with melted butter. Yield: 32 servings.

Note: This recipe also works well using half white and half white whole-wheat flour.

Nutrition Facts	
Amount Per Serving	
Calories 180 (23% from Fat, 11% from Protein, 67% from Carb)	
Total Fat 4 g	
Saturated Fat 1 g	
Mono Fat 2 g	
Cholesterol 31 mg	
Sodium 121 mg	
Total Carbohydrate 29 g	
Dietary Fiber 1 g	
Sugars 2 g	
Protein 5 g	
Calcium 9 mg	
Iron 2 mg	

Sourdough Pretzels

1 tbsp. butter
1½ tbsp. sugar
1 tsp. salt
½ cup hot water
¾ cup Basic Sourdough Batter
1⅜ cups white flour
1⅜ cups white whole-wheat flour
1 egg yolk
Kosher salt, optional
Sesame seeds, optional

Add butter, sugar, and salt to hot water, and let it come to lukewarm.

After water mixture has cooled, add to batter. Mix together the flours. Add 2 cups flour ¼ cup at a time, stirring after each addition. Turn out onto a floured board and knead in ¾ cup more flour. Dough will be very stiff.

Place dough in a greased bowl. Turn over in bowl, cover, and let sit 2 hours.

On a clean board (no flour), break off pieces of dough about the size of an egg. Roll in palm of hand into 18-in. pieces about ½ in. in diameter. Twist into pretzel shapes.

Place on greased baking sheet. Brush with egg yolk mixed with a little water. Sprinkle with kosher salt and/or sesame seeds. Cover and place in a warm spot for 30 minutes.

Bake approximately 15 min. in a pre-heated 425-degree oven. Yield: 18 servings.

Nutrition Facts
Amount Per Serving
Calories 91 (12% from Fat, 12% from Protein, 77% from Carb)
Total Fat 1 g
Saturated Fat 1 g
Mono Fat 0 g
Cholesterol 13 mg
Sodium 137 mg
Total Carbohydrate 18 g
Dietary Fiber 1 g
Sugars 1 g
Protein 3 g
Calcium 7 mg
Iron 1 mg

Sourdough Chocolate Cake

1 cup trans-fat-free shortening
1 cup sugar
2 eggs
1 cup Basic Sourdough Batter
1 cup buttermilk
3 squares unsweetened chocolate, melted
1 tsp vanilla extract
½ tsp cinnamon
½ tsp. salt
1½ tsp. baking soda
2 cups flour
Chocolate Glaze (see index)

With electric mixer, cream together shortening and sugar until light and fluffy. Beat in eggs, 1 at a time. Stir in batter, buttermilk, chocolate, vanilla, and cinnamon; beat with mixer 2 min.

Mix together salt and baking soda and sprinkle over batter. Fold in gently. Stir in flour until batter is smooth.

Pour batter into a greased 9x13-in. baking pan. Bake in a preheated 350-degree oven 30-40 min. or until toothpick inserted in center comes out clean. Cool. Drizzle Chocolate Glaze over cake. Yield: 16 servings.

Nutrition Facts
Amount Per Serving
Calories 279 (49% from Fat, 5% from Protein, 46% from Carb)
Total Fat 15 g
Saturated Fat 4 g
Mono Fat 7 g
Cholesterol 31 mg
Sodium 209 mg
Total Carbohydrate 32 g
Dietary Fiber 1 g
Sugars 16 g
Protein 4 g
Calcium 21 mg
Iron 1 mg

Chapter 7

Tea Breads and Yeast Breads

Tea breads are quick breads. They do not require yeast to leaven and rise and do not have to be kneaded. They can be made quickly with the addition of baking powder or baking soda. Tea breads are not as sweet as cake, and they do not require frosting. They also bake well with blended flours. With just a little spread of softened butter or cream cheese, they're ready to be enjoyed by the slice. Tea breads are an afternoon delight, served properly on fine china with a cup of cinnamon tea. One of my most popular recipes happens to be a tea bread—Best Banana Bread. Look for the recipe in this chapter. I also include 2 yeast recipes here.

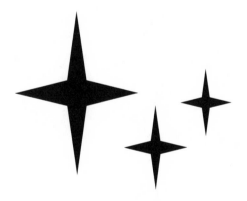

Mango Bread

½ cup white flour

½ cup white whole-wheat or whole-wheat flour

½ cup soy flour

½ cup oat flour

2 tsp. cinnamon

2 tsp. baking soda

1 tsp. baking powder

3 eggs

¼ cup butter, melted

½ cup canola oil

1 cup sugar

2 large mangos, peeled and pitted

½ cup walnuts, chopped

½ cup shredded coconut

In medium bowl, sift together flours, cinnamon, baking soda, and baking powder.

In large bowl, beat together eggs, butter, oil, and sugar. Add flour mixture and blend.

Mash 1 mango, and roughly dice the other. Fold mango, coconut, and nuts into batter.

Spread batter into 2 9x5-in. loaf pans that have been greased and floured on the bottoms only. Bake 50 min. in a preheated 350-degree oven, or until toothpick inserted in centers comes out clean. Let cool 10 min. before removing from pans. Cool completely on wire rack. Yield: 32 servings.

Nutrition Facts		
Amount Per Serving		
Calories 125 (51% from Fat, 7% from Protein, 42% from Carb)		
Total Fat 7 g		
Saturated Fat 2 g		
Mono Fat 3 g		
Cholesterol 27 mg		
Sodium 115 mg		
Total Carbohydrate 14 g		
Dietary Fiber 1 g		
Sugars 9 g		
Protein 2 g		
Calcium 21 mg		
Iron 1 mg		

Blueberry-Pumpkin Bread

STREUSEL TOPPING:

2 tbsp. flour

2 tbsp. sugar

¼ tsp. cinnamon

1 tbsp. butter

BREAD:

1 cup all-purpose flour

⅔ cup white whole-wheat or oat flour

1 tsp. baking soda

½ tsp. baking powder

½ tsp. salt

1 tsp. cinnamon

½ tsp. allspice

1 cup pumpkin, firmly packed

¼ cup evaporated milk

⅓ cup Canola Butter (see index) or Smart Balance® regular spread

½ cup brown sugar, firmly packed

1 egg

1 cup blueberries

1 tbsp. flour

Combine dry streusel ingredients. Cut in butter until crumbly. Set aside.

Combine first 7 bread ingredients. In separate bowl, combine pumpkin and milk until blended.

With mixer in large mixing bowl, cream butter and sugar. Add egg, and beat until fluffy. Add flour mixture alternately with pumpkin mixture, beating well after each addition.

Combine blueberries and flour. Gently stir into batter. Pour into a 9x5-in. loaf pan that has been greased and floured on the

Nutrition Facts
Amount Per Serving
Calories 148 (35% from Fat, 7% from Protein, 58% from Carb)
Total Fat 6 g
Saturated Fat 2 g
Mono Fat 2 g
Cholesterol 23 mg
Sodium 200 mg
Total Carbohydrate 22 g
Dietary Fiber 2 g
Sugars 10 g
Protein 3 g
Calcium 38 mg
Iron 1 mg

bottom only, and sprinkle with streusel topping. Bake 1 hour at 350 degrees, or until toothpick inserted in center comes out clean.

Cool in pan 10 min. Invert and cool completely on wire rack. Good served with Canola Butter or cream cheese. Yield: 16 servings.

Strawberry Bread

½ cup oat flour
½ cup soy flour
½ white flour
½ tsp. baking soda
½ tsp. cinnamon
½ cup sugar
2 eggs, beaten
1 (10-oz.) box frozen strawberries with juice, thawed
¾ cup canola oil
½ cup pecans or walnuts, chopped

Sift together flours, baking soda, cinnamon, and sugar. Combine eggs, strawberries, and oil. Add to flour mixture. Mix in nuts.

Pour into a 9x5-in. loaf pan that has been greased and floured on the bottom only. Bake 1 hour in a preheated 325-degree oven, or until toothpick inserted in center comes out clean. Remove from pan after 10 min., and let cool completely before slicing. Serve with light cream cheese or Canola Butter (see index). Yield: 16 servings.

Note: You may substitute 2 cups sliced strawberries, sweetened to taste with Splenda®, for frozen berries.

Nutrition Facts		
Amount Per Serving		
Calories 354 (34% from Fat, 4% from Protein, 62% from Carb)		
Total Fat 14 g		
Saturated Fat 1 g		
Mono Fat 8 g		
Cholesterol 31 mg		
Sodium 55 mg		
Total Carbohydrate 58 g		
Dietary Fiber 4 g		
Sugars 49 g		
Protein 4 g		
Calcium 35 mg		
Iron 2 mg		

Cranberry Bread

½ cup white flour
½ cup white wholewheat flour
½ cup soy flour
½ cup oat flour
1½ tsp. baking powder
½ tsp. baking soda
1 tsp. salt
Juice and zest of 1 orange
2 tbsp. trans-fat-free shortening
Boiling water
1 egg, beaten
¾ cup sugar
1 cup walnuts, chopped
1 cup raw cranberries, halved

Sift together flours, baking powder, baking soda, and salt. Combine orange juice, zest, and shortening with enough boiling water to yield ¾ cup. Cool slightly and add egg and sugar. Add to flour mixture, stirring just until combined. Blend in walnuts and cranberries.

Pour into 2 9x5-in. loaf pans that have been greased and floured on the bottoms only. Bake approximately 40 min. in a preheated 350-degree oven, or until toothpick inserted in centers comes out clean. Cool in pan 10 min. Remove and cool completely on wire rack. Yield: 32 servings.

Nutrition Facts

Amount Per Serving

Calories 81 (39% from Fat, 11% from Protein, 50% from Carb)

Total Fat 4 g	
Saturated Fat 0 g	
Mono Fat 1 g	
Cholesterol 8 mg	
Sodium 180 mg	
Total Carbohydrate 11 g	
Dietary Fiber 1 g	
Sugars 6 g	
Protein 2 g	
Calcium 57 mg	
Iron 1 mg	

Best Banana Bread

1 cup oat flour
½ cup whole-wheat flour
½ cup all-purpose flour
½ cup sugar
¾ tsp. baking soda
½ tsp. salt
1 cup toasted pecans or walnuts, chopped
3 very ripe bananas, mashed (about 1½ cups)
¼ cup plain yogurt
2 large eggs, lightly beaten
6 tbsp. canola oil
1 tsp. vanilla extract

Combine dry ingredients. In separate bowl, combine wet ingredients. Lightly fold wet ingredients into dry ingredients with spatula just until combined.

Grease and flour bottom only of 9x5-in. loaf pan. Pour batter into pan. Bake approximately 55 min. in a preheated 350-degree oven, or until toothpick inserted in center comes out clean.

Cool 5 min. and invert. Cool completely on wire rack. Store in refrigerator up to 4 days or on counter up to 2 days. Yield: 16 servings.

Nutrition Facts

Amount Per Serving

Calories 201 (49% from Fat, 7% from Protein, 44% from Carb)

Total Fat 11 g	
Saturated Fat 1 g	
Mono Fat 6 g	
Cholesterol 31 mg	
Sodium 146 mg	
Total Carbohydrate 23 g	
Dietary Fiber 3 g	
Sugars 10 g	
Protein 4 g	
Calcium 23 mg	
Iron 1 mg	

Gingerbread

2 eggs

½ cup sugar

½ cup molasses

¾ cup melted Canola Butter (see index) or Smart Balance® regular spread

1¼ cups whole-wheat pastry flour

1¼ cups white flour

2 tsp. baking powder

2 tsp. ginger

1½ tsp. cinnamon

½ tsp. ground cloves

½ tsp. nutmeg

½ tsp. baking soda

½ tsp. salt

1 cup boiling water

Beat eggs. Blend in sugar, molasses, and butter or spread. Sift together flours, baking powder, spices, baking soda, and salt. Alternate adding flour mixture with water to batter, and beat until smooth.

Pour into a greased 9-in. square baking pan. Bake 30-40 min. in a preheated 350-degree oven, or until toothpick inserted in center comes out clean. Serve warm with whipped cream. Yield: 9 servings.

Nutrition Facts	
Amount Per Serving	
Calories 374 (40% from Fat, 6% from Protein, 54% from Carb)	
Total Fat 17 g	
Saturated Fat 6 g	
Mono Fat 7 g	
Cholesterol 71 mg	
Sodium 506 mg	
Total Carbohydrate 51 g	
Dietary Fiber 3 g	
Sugars 22 g	
Protein 6 g	
Calcium 124 mg	
Iron 3 mg	

Peanut Butter Bread

¾ cup water

1 cup bread flour

1 cup white whole-wheat flour

2½ tbsp. brown sugar

¼ tsp. salt

⅓ cup plain or crunchy peanut butter

2 tsp. active dry yeast

Add ingredients to bread maker in order recommended in the manual. Bake according to bread maker directions. Yield: 16 servings.

Nutrition Facts
Amount Per Serving
Calories 97 (28% from Fat, 14% from Protein, 59% from Carb)
Total Fat 3 g
Saturated Fat 1 g
Mono Fat 1 g
Cholesterol 0 mg
Sodium 65 mg
Total Carbohydrate 15 g
Dietary Fiber 1 g
Sugars 3 g
Protein 3 g
Calcium 8 mg
Iron 1 mg

Herbed Whole-Wheat Pizza Dough

1 (¼-oz.) pkg. active dry yeast
1 tsp. sugar
1 cup warm water
2 cups whole-wheat or white whole-wheat flour
¼ cup wheat germ
1 tsp. salt
2 tsp. Italian seasonings
1 tbsp. olive oil or canola oil

In small bowl, dissolve yeast and sugar in warm water. Let sit 10 min.

In large bowl, combine flour, wheat germ, salt, and seasonings. Make a well in center and add yeast mixture and oil. Stir well to combine. Cover and let rise a few minutes.

Roll dough out on a greased 16-in. pizza pan and poke a few holes with a fork. Let dough rise again 10 min.

Bake 15 min. in a preheated 350-degree oven. Add desired sauce and toppings, and bake again until desired crispness. Yield: 12 servings.

Nutrition Facts		
Amount Per		
Calories 88 (17% from Fat, 14% from Protein, 69% from Carb)		
Total Fat 2 g		
Saturated Fat 0 g		
Mono Fat 1 g		
Cholesterol 0 mg		
Sodium 198 mg		
Total Carbohydrate 16 g		
Dietary Fiber 3 g		
Sugars 0 g		
Protein 3 g		
Calcium 8 mg		
Iron 1 mg		

Chapter 8

Cakes and Tortes

Most celebrations call for cake. But cakes can be cloyingly sweet and high in carbs, especially when traditional frosting—with 2 to 3 cups powdered sugar—is used. Fortunately, there are many types of cake recipes to choose from: layer cakes, angel food cakes, nut cakes, Bundt cakes, upside-down cakes, rolled cakes, flourless cakes, tortes, pound cakes, cheesecakes, cupcakes, etc. Choose wisely and you can have your cake and eat it too.

Nut-cake bases are typically low carb. Angel food cakes, flourless cakes, pound cakes, and cheesecakes do not require frostings. Spread thin layers of frosting on your other cakes, or choose low-impact toppings such as a light sprinkling of powdered sugar, a glaze, or a dollop of whipped cream. At the end of this chapter, I have included low-sugar frostings and cake toppings. If you mix your flours, reduce the sugar, and pay attention to portion size, you'll no longer have to sneak your desserts!

Pound cakes can be a bit high in carbs. All of the pound cakes in this chapter can be made using half all-purpose flour and half almond flour to lessen the carbs. For instance, the 7Up® Pound Cake will have approximately 10 fewer carbs per serving with this substitution.

Note: Bundt pans generally have fluted or molded sides, and tube pans have straight sides. They can be used interchangeably, although chiffon and angel food cakes typically are baked in tube pans.

Flourless Chocolate Cake

8 oz. sugar-free or bittersweet chocolate, coarsely chopped
½ cup butter, cut into pieces and softened
2 whole eggs
4 separated eggs
1 cup sugar or Splenda®
1 tsp. vanilla extract

Melt chocolate in double boiler or bowl set over hot water. Remove from heat and whisk in butter until it melts; set aside.

In a bowl, whisk whole eggs and 4 egg yolks with ½ cup sugar or Splenda® and the vanilla, just until blended. Whisk in warm chocolate mixture.

In separate bowl with an electric mixer, beat egg whites until foamy. Slowly add remaining sugar or Splenda®. Beat until whites form soft peaks that hold their shape but are not quite stiff. Stir approximately ¼ of beaten whites into chocolate mixture to lighten it. Gently fold in remaining whites.

Pour batter into an 8-in. springform pan that has been lined on the bottom with a round of wax paper. Smooth top of batter and place pan in a preheated 350-degree oven. Bake until top of cake is puffed and cracked and center is firm, approximately 35-40 min. Do not overbake.

Cool cake on a wire rack. Center of cake will fall as it cools. At serving time, fill center with sweetened whipped cream and dust top lightly with sifted cocoa. Run tip of a knife around edges of cake, and carefully remove sides of pan. Yield: 8-12 servings.

Nutrition Facts

Amount Per Serving

Calories 271 (61% from Fat, 8% from Protein, 30% from Carb)

Total Fat 20 g	
Saturated Fat 12 g	
Mono Fat 6 g	
Cholesterol 143 mg	
Sodium 100 mg	
Total Carbohydrate 23 g	
Dietary Fiber 3 g	
Sugars 17 g	
Protein 6 g	
Calcium 37 mg	
Iron 4 mg	

Red Velvet Cake

CAKE:

1¼ cups sugar

½ cup shortening

2 eggs

2 tbsp. cocoa powder

2 oz. red food coloring

1¼ cups cake flour

1 cup white whole-wheat flour

1 tsp. salt

1 cup buttermilk

1 tsp. vanilla extract

1 tbsp. vinegar

1 tsp. baking soda

CREAM CHEESE FROSTING:

1 (1.5-oz.) pkg. vanilla sugar-free pudding mix

1¾ cups milk

1 (8-oz.) pkg. regular or light cream cheese, softened

1 (8-oz.) pkg. whipped topping, thawed

Cream sugar and shortening together. Add eggs and beat well. Make a paste of cocoa and food coloring and add to creamed mixture.

Sift together flours and salt. Add buttermilk alternately with flours to creamed mixture. Add vanilla.

Put vinegar in a deep bowl and add baking soda. Mixture will foam. Once blended, add to cake batter. Blend well but do not beat.

Pour batter into 2 greased and floured 9-in. cake pans. Bake 25-30 min. in a preheated 350-degree oven, or until toothpick inserted in centers comes out clean. Cool.

For the frosting, in medium bowl, combine pudding mix and milk well. Let stand until thickened.

Nutrition Facts	
Amount Per Serving	
Calories 307 (48% from Fat, 7% from Protein, 45% from Carb)	
Total Fat 17 g	
Saturated Fat 9 g	
Mono Fat 5 g	
Cholesterol 49 mg	
Sodium 327 mg	
Total Carbohydrate 35 g	
Dietary Fiber 1 g	
Sugars 21 g	
Protein 5 g	
Calcium 53 mg	
Iron 2 mg	

In large bowl, beat cream cheese until smooth. Add milk mixture and mix well. Fold in whipped topping.

Frost cooled cake between the 2 layers and on top and sides. Yield: 16 servings.

Spanish Bar Cake

2 cups water
1 cup raisins
½ cup trans-fat-free shortening
¾ cup sugar
1 tsp. baking soda
1 cup white flour
1 cup white whole-wheat flour
½ tsp. ground cloves
½ tsp. cinnamon
½ tsp. nutmeg
½ tsp. allspice
¼ tsp. salt
1 large egg, beaten
½ cup walnuts, chopped
Cream Cheese Frosting (see index)

Combine water and raisins in saucepan. Heat to boiling and simmer 10 min. Add shortening and allow mixture to cool.

While raisins are simmering, sift together sugar, soda, flours, spices, and salt.

Add cooled raisin mixture to flour mixture and blend well. Add egg and stir well. Fold in walnuts.

Spread batter in a greased 4x8-in. loaf pan. Bake approximately 40 min. at 350 degrees, or until toothpick inserted in center comes out clean. Cool in pan 10 min. Remove from pan and cool completely on wire rack. Frost with Cream Cheese Frosting. Yield: 16 servings.

Nutrition Facts

Amount Per Serving

Calories 208 (39% from Fat, 7% from Protein, 55% from Carb)

Total Fat 9 g	
Saturated Fat 2 g	
Mono Fat 4 g	
Cholesterol 15 mg	
Sodium 123 mg	
Total Carbohydrate 30 g	
Dietary Fiber 2 g	
Sugars 16 g	
Protein 4 g	
Calcium 15 mg	
Iron 1 mg	

Burnt Almond Torte

CUSTARD CREAM:

1 cup milk

3 large egg yolks

¼ cup Splenda®

2 tbsp. cornstarch

1 tbsp. butter

½ tsp. vanilla extract

⅓ cup whipping cream

1 tbsp. powdered sugar

TORTE:

¾ cup cake flour

½ cup white whole-wheat flour

¾ tsp. baking powder

¼ tsp. baking soda

¼ tsp. salt

6 tbsp. butter, softened

⅔ cup sugar

2 eggs

½ cup buttermilk

¾ tsp. vanilla extract

ALMOND BRITTLE:

¼ cup Splenda®

¼ cup sugar

3 tbsp. honey

1½ tbsp. water

½ cup slivered almonds, toasted in oven and cooled

1 tbsp. butter

⅛ tsp. baking soda

Make custard cream the night before and chill. To make custard cream, in heavy saucepan over medium-low heat, heat milk just to simmering. Meanwhile, with whisk in medium bowl, blend egg yolks, Splenda®, and cornstarch. Stir heated milk into egg mixture, and return mixture to saucepan. Bring back to a boil over medium-low heat, whisking constantly. Boil 1 min. Remove pan from heat and add butter and vanilla. Pour through strainer. Transfer custard to a bowl, and add a piece of waxed paper or plastic wrap directly on top to prevent a skin from forming. Refrigerate until cold.

Once custard is cold, whip cream and powdered sugar until stiff peaks form. Fold into chilled custard and refrigerate until ready to use.

For torte, all ingredients should be at room temperature.

In small bowl, sift together dry ingredients and set aside.

With electric mixer at medium speed, cream together butter and sugar until light and fluffy. Reduce speed to medium low. Add eggs 1 at a time, beating after each addition. Alternately add flour mixture and buttermilk and vanilla, blending well after each addition.

Pour batter into a greased 8x2-in. round cake pan. Bake approximately 30 min. in a preheated 350-degree oven, or until toothpick inserted in center comes out clean. Cool in pan 10 min. Remove from pan and cool completely on wire rack.

For almond brittle, combine Splenda®, sugar, honey, and water in medium saucepan. Bring to a boil over medium heat, stirring to dissolve Splenda® and sugar. Boil, without stirring, until mixture turns a deep amber color, about 10 min. Remove pan from heat and immediately stir in almonds, butter, and baking soda. With a wooden spoon, mix just until butter melts and foam subsides. Pour this mixture onto a lightly greased baking sheet and set aside to cool. When brittle has hardened, break up and place in a food processor, crushing to fine crumbs. Store in a covered container in the refrigerator until ready to use.

Assemble torte by cutting cake in half horizontally. Place a layer on a cake plate, and spread the top of the layer with some cold custard cream. Sprinkle with some crushed brittle, reserving remainder for top and sides. Place remaining cake layer on top. Spread remaining custard cream over torte, applying a thinner coat to the sides, then the top. Chill for at least 1 hour before garnishing.

To garnish, press some remaining brittle crumbs onto sides of torte with palm of your hand, and sprinkle a layer of crumbs on top. Refrigerate until ready to serve. Yield: 16 servings.

Nutrition Facts

Amount Per Serving

Calories 214 (44% from Fat, 7% from Protein, 48% from Carb)

Total Fat 11 g
  Saturated Fat 5 g
  Mono Fat 4 g
Cholesterol 88 mg
Sodium 151 mg
Total Carbohydrate 26 g
  Dietary Fiber 1 g
  Sugars 16 g
Protein 4 g
Calcium 50 mg
Iron 1 mg

Tres Leches Cake

CAKE:

¾ cup cake flour

¾ cup white whole-wheat flour

1½ tsp. baking powder

1 cup sugar

8 tbsp. butter, Canola Butter (see index), or Smart Balance® regular spread

5 eggs

1½ tsp. vanilla extract

SOAKING SYRUP:

1 cup milk

1¾ cups Sugar-Free Sweetened Condensed Milk (see index)

1 (5-oz.) can evaporated skim milk

TOPPING:

1½ cups sugar-free whipped cream or whipped topping, thawed

GARNISH:

Fruit of your choice (sliced strawberries, pineapple, peaches, cherries, etc.)

For cake, combine flours and baking powder and set aside.

With mixer on medium speed, beat sugar and butter or butter substitute until light and fluffy. Add eggs 1 at a time, beating well after each addition. Add vanilla. Gently fold in flour mixture; do not overmix. Spread into 9x13-in. greased and floured baking pan and bake approximately 30 min. at 350 degrees.

For soaking syrup, mix together milks. Pierce warm cake with fork at ½-in. intervals. Pour milk mixture slowly over cake. Mixture will be slowly absorbed. Cool cake completely at room temperature.

Cover cake with plastic wrap and place in refrigerator for several hours or up to 1 day. Just before serving, frost with whipped cream or topping and garnish. Store in refrigerator. Yield: 16 servings.

Nutrition Facts
Amount Per Serving
Calories 199 (43% from Fat, 9% from Protein, 47% from Carb)
Total Fat 10 g
Saturated Fat 5 g
Mono Fat 3 g
Cholesterol 99 mg
Sodium 249 mg
Total Carbohydrate 24 g
Dietary Fiber 1 g
Sugars 14 g
Protein 5 g
Calcium 145 mg
Iron 1 mg

Orange Marmalade Linzer Torte

10 tbsp. butter, softened
⅓ cup sugar
1¼ cups flour
1 cup ground almonds
1 tsp. lemon zest
¼ tsp. cinnamon
⅛ tsp. nutmeg
2 raw egg yolks
2 hardboiled egg yolks
1 tsp. vanilla extract
1 (15.5-oz.) jar low-sugar orange marmalade
1 egg white, beaten
Slivered almonds

In mixing bowl with mixer at medium speed, combine butter and sugar until fluffy. Add flour, ground almonds, lemon zest, cinnamon, nutmeg, raw egg yolks, boiled egg yolks, and vanilla. Continue to mix until well combined. Chill for at least 1 hour.

Divide chilled dough into 2 pieces. Roll out 1 piece, and fit into a greased 8x8-in. pan or springform pan. Spread marmalade over dough with a spatula.

With the remaining dough, make a lattice top to cover marmalade. Brush with egg white and sprinkle almonds on top. Bake approximately 45 min. at 350 degrees, or until crust is a pale golden color. Yield: 9 servings.

Nutrition Facts
Amount Per Serving
Calories 294 (46% from Fat, 7% from Protein, 47% from Carb)
Total Fat 17 g
Saturated Fat 7 g
Mono Fat 7 g
Cholesterol 100 mg
Sodium 91 mg
Total Carbohydrate 39 g
Dietary Fiber 2 g
Sugars 20 g
Protein 6 g
Calcium 41 mg
Iron 2 mg

Carrot Torte

1½ cups sugar
1½ cups canola oil
4 large eggs
1 cup cake flour
½ cup oat flour
½ cup white whole-wheat flour
2 tsp. baking powder
2 tsp. baking soda
1 tsp. salt
1 tsp. cinnamon
¾ tsp. nutmeg
3 cups finely grated peeled carrots
½ cup pecans, chopped
½ cup raisins
Cream Cheese Frosting (see index for Red Velvet Cake)

With mixer, beat together sugar and oil until combined. Add eggs 1 at a time, beating well after each.

Sift together flours, baking powder, baking soda, salt, cinnamon, and nutmeg. Add to sugar and oil mixture.

Stir in carrots, pecans, and raisins.

Pour batter into 3 9-in. cake pans that have been lined on the bottoms with lightly greased waxed paper. Bake approximately 45 min. at 325 degrees. Cool in pans 10 min. Remove from pans, peel off waxed paper, and cool layers completely on wire rack.

Frost top of each layer with Cream Cheese Frosting, and assemble like a torte. Yield: 16 servings.

Nutrition Facts	
Amount Per Serving	
Calories 378 (58% from Fat, 4% from Protein, 38% from Carb)	
Total Fat 25 g	
Saturated Fat 2 g	
Mono Fat 14 g	
Cholesterol 61 mg	
Sodium 398 mg	
Total Carbohydrate 37 g	
Dietary Fiber 2 g	
Sugars 23 g	
Protein 4 g	
Calcium 58 mg	
Iron 2 mg	

Healthy Carrot Cake

2 tbsp. canola oil

2 eggs, beaten

1 cup unsweetened applesauce

1 cup shredded carrots

1½ cups white whole-wheat or whole-wheat flour

½ tsp. salt

½ tsp. baking powder

½ tsp. baking soda

1½ tsp. cinnamon

1 tsp. vanilla extract

2 tbsp. chopped walnuts or pecans

4 tbsp. brown sugar

¼ cup water

4 tbsp. raisins

Combine all ingredients. Pour into a greased 9-in. cake pan. Bake 30 min. in a preheated 350-degree oven.

Cool in pan 10 min. Remove from pan and cool completely on wire rack. Serve with whipped topping, if desired. Yield: 8 servings.

Nutrition Facts
Amount Per Serving
Calories 201 (28% from Fat, 11% from Protein, 61% from Carb)
Total Fat 6 g
Saturated Fat 1 g
Mono Fat 3 g
Cholesterol 61 mg
Sodium 289 mg
Total Carbohydrate 32 g
Dietary Fiber 4 g
Sugars 10 g
Protein 6 g
Calcium 52 mg
Iron 2 mg

Chocolate Zucchini Bundt Cake

½ cup canola oil
1 tsp. vanilla extract
1 cup sugar
½ cup Splenda®
2 eggs
½ cup milk
1 tsp. baking soda
1¼ cups white flour
1¼ cups white whole-wheat or whole-wheat flour
¼ cup cocoa powder
½ tsp. cinnamon
½ tsp. nutmeg
½ tsp. salt
2 cups grated zucchini

Combine oil, vanilla, sugar, Splenda®, eggs, and milk. Sift together baking soda, flours, cocoa, cinnamon, nutmeg, and salt. Add dry ingredients alternately with zucchini to wet mixture.

Pour batter into a greased Bundt pan. Bake approximately 60-65 min. in a preheated 350-degree oven. Cool in pan 10 min. Unmold and cool completely on wire rack. Yield: 16 servings.

Nutrition Facts	
Amount Per Serving	
Calories 204 (35% from Fat, 8% from Protein, 57% from Carb)	
Total Fat 8 g	
Saturated Fat 1 g	
Mono Fat 4 g	
Cholesterol 31 mg	
Sodium 175 mg	
Total Carbohydrate 30 g	
Dietary Fiber 2 g	
Sugars 14 g	
Protein 4 g	
Calcium 37 mg	
Iron 2 mg	

Earl Grey Bundt Cake with Chocolate Sauce

CAKE:
4 bags Earl Grey tea
⅓ cup boiling water
1 cup cake flour
1 cup white whole-wheat flour
½ tsp. baking powder
¼ tsp. salt
⅓ cup cocoa powder
1 cup butter or Smart Balance® regular spread, softened
1 cup sugar
1 cup Splenda®
4 large eggs
⅓ cup milk
1 tsp. vanilla extract
Powdered sugar

CHOCOLATE SAUCE:
¾ cup whipping cream
3 bags Earl Grey tea
8 oz. bittersweet chocolate, chopped
2 tbsp. light corn syrup

For cake, place tea bags in glass measuring cup. Pour boiling water over and steep 8 min. Remove and discard tea bags; cool tea completely.

Combine flours, baking powder, salt, and cocoa and set aside.

With mixer on medium speed, beat butter 2 min. until creamy. Gradually add sugar and Splenda®, beating 5-7 minutes. Add eggs 1 at a time, beating just until yellow disappears. Set aside.

Stir together milk and tea. Alternately add flour mixture to butter mixture, beginning and ending with flour and mixing at low speed after each addition, just until blended. Stir in vanilla extract.

Pour batter into a greased and floured 10-cup Bundt pan. Bake 1 hour and 15 min. in a preheated oven, or until toothpick inserted in center comes out clean. Cool 15 min. before unmolding from pan.

Cool completely on wire rack. Dust with powdered sugar. Yield: 12 servings.

For chocolate sauce, in small heavy saucepan over medium heat, heat cream until hot but not boiling, stirring often. Remove from heat. Add tea bags to hot cream, cover, and steep 5 min. Remove and discard tea bags. Add chocolate and corn syrup and stir until chocolate melts. Serve with cake. Yield: 1½ cups.

Nutrition Facts

Amount Per Serving

Calories 333 (50% from Fat, 6% from Protein, 44% from Carb)

Total Fat 19 g	
Saturated Fat 12 g	
Mono Fat 6 g	
Cholesterol 98 mg	
Sodium 163 mg	
Total Carbohydrate 39 g	
Dietary Fiber 2 g	
Sugars 23 g	
Protein 5 g	
Calcium 37 mg	
Iron 2 mg	

Rose Petal Cake

CAKE:

1 cup sugar

Petals of 6 red organic roses

½ cup butter, softened

4 eggs, separated

2 tsp. lemon zest

2½ tbsp. orange zest

1 tsp. rose water

1¼ cups cake flour

1 cup white whole-wheat flour

1½ tsp. baking powder

1 tsp. baking soda

1 cup buttermilk

⅔ cup pistachio nuts, chopped

Edible roses for garnish

GLAZE:

3 tbsp. milk

1¼ cups Splenda®

1-2 tsp. rose water

For cake, blend sugar in blender until superfine consistency; set aside.

Gently wash and dry rose petals. Snip only red part of petals into small pieces; set aside.

Cream butter and add sugar, beating until light and smooth. Add egg yolks, zests, and rose water, mixing well.

Sift flours, baking powder, and baking soda together. Add alternately with buttermilk to creamed mixture. Fold in rose petals.

Beat egg whites until stiff, and gently fold into mixture.

Sprinkle half the pistachios on bottom of a greased and floured 2-qt. tube pan. Pour batter on top and sprinkle with remaining nuts.

Bake 40 min. in a preheated 350-degree oven, or until cake springs back when touched. Cool in pan 10 min. Remove from pan and cool completely on wire rack.

For glaze, add milk to Splenda®. Add rose water. Drizzle on warm cake. Garnish cake with edible roses. Yield: 16 servings.

Note: Rose petals will become dark green after baking.

Nutrition Facts	
Amount Per Serving of Cake	
Calories 219 (40% from Fat, 9% from Protein, 51% from Carb)	
Total Fat 10 g	
Saturated Fat 5 g	
Mono Fat 3 g	
Cholesterol 77 mg	
Sodium 193 mg	
Total Carbohydrate 28 g	
Dietary Fiber 2 g	
Sugars 14 g	
Protein 5 g	
Calcium 56 mg	
Iron 2 mg	

Nutrition Facts	
Amount Per Recipe of Glaze	
Calories 147 Cal (9% from Fat, 4% from Protein, 87% from Carb)	
Total Fat 1 g	
Saturated Fat 1 g	
Mono Fat 0 g	
Cholesterol 5 mg	
Sodium 18 mg	
Total Carbohydrate 32 g	
Dietary Fiber 0 g	
Sugars 2 g	
Protein 1 g	
Calcium 52 mg	
Iron 0 mg	

Irish Whiskey Bundt Cake

1 (18.25-oz.) pkg. yellow cake mix, regular or reduced sugar

1 (1.5-oz.) pkg. sugar-free chocolate pudding mix

¾ cup canola oil

¼ cup water

¼ cup Irish whiskey

¼ cup Irish cream liqueur

4 eggs

In bowl with electric mixer, combine all ingredients. Beat until smooth. Pour batter into a greased and floured 10-in. or 12-cup Bundt pan.

Bake 40-50 min. in a preheated 350-degree oven, or until toothpick inserted in center comes out clean. Cool in pan 10 min. Unmold and cool completely on wire rack. Yield: 10 servings.

Nutrition Facts
Amount Per Serving
Calories 442 (49% from Fat, 5% from Protein, 46% from Carb)
Total Fat 23 g
Saturated Fat 3 g
Mono Fat 11 g
Cholesterol 98 mg
Sodium 427 mg
Total Carbohydrate 49 g
Dietary Fiber 0 g
Sugars 26 g
Protein 5 g
Calcium 99 mg
Iron 1 mg

Apricot Brandy Bundt Cake

CAKE:

1 cup butter or Smart Balance® regular spread, softened

1½ cups Splenda®

1½ cups sugar

6 eggs

1 cup regular or light sour cream

1 tsp. orange extract

1 tsp. lemon extract

1 tsp. almond extract

¼ cup apricot brandy

1½ cups cake flour

1½ cups white whole-wheat flour

Nutrition Facts		
Amount Per Serving of Cake		
Calories 338 (45% from Fat, 7% from Protein, 48% from Carb)		
Total Fat 17 g		
Saturated Fat 10 g		
Mono Fat 5 g		
Cholesterol 129 mg		
Sodium 121 mg		
Total Carbohydrate 41 g		
Dietary Fiber 2 g		
Sugars 19 g		
Protein 6 g		
Calcium 38 mg		
Iron 2 mg		

GLAZE:

½ cup no-sugar-added apricot preserves

1 tbsp. apricot brandy or apricot nectar

1 (8-oz.) can apricot halves, drained

Mint leaves for garnish

For cake, cream butter. Gradually add Splenda® and sugar and continue creaming until light and fluffy. Add eggs 1 at a time, beating well after each addition.

In small bowl, combine sour cream, extracts, and brandy.

Combine flours. Add flours alternately with sour cream mixture to creamed butter mixture. Beat until smooth and well combined.

Pour cake batter into a greased and floured 10-in. or 12-cup Bundt pan. Bake 1½ hours in a preheated 325-degree oven, or until toothpick inserted in center comes out clean. Cool in pan 10 min. Unmold and cool completely on wire rack before glazing.

For glaze, heat preserves until melted.

Nutrition Facts		
Amount Per Recipe of Glaze		
Calories 388 (1% from Fat, 1% from Protein, 98% from Carb)		
Total Fat 0 g		
Saturated Fat 0 g		
Mono Fat 0 g		
Cholesterol 0 mg		
Sodium 31 mg		
Total Carbohydrate 118 g		
Dietary Fiber 6 g		
Sugars 43 g		
Protein 2 g		
Calcium 29 mg		
Iron 2 mg		

Remove from heat. Stir in brandy or nectar. Spread warm glaze over cake. Place apricot halves and mint leaves around base of cake for garnish. Yield: 16 servings.

Clove Bundt Cake

1 cup butter or Smart Balance® regular spread, softened
1¼ cups sugar
5 eggs
1 cup cake flour
1 cup white whole-wheat flour
1 tbsp. ground cloves
1 tbsp. cinnamon
Pinch salt
1 tbsp. baking soda
1 cup buttermilk

Cream together butter and sugar. Beat in eggs 1 at a time. Set aside.

Sift flours with cloves, cinnamon, and salt and set aside.

Stir baking soda into ⅓ of the buttermilk. Add this to butter batter, mixing well.

Add remaining buttermilk alternately with flour mixture to batter, beating well.

Pour batter into a greased 10-in. or 12-cup Bundt pan. Bake 45-50 min. in a preheated 350-degree oven. Cool 10 min. and unmold from pan. Cool completely on wire rack. Dust with powdered sugar, pour on a light glaze, or serve with whipped cream. Yield: 16 servings.

Note: Clove cake was a favorite of Pres. Theodore Roosevelt.

Nutrition Facts
Amount Per Serving
Calories 252 (48% from Fat, 7% from Protein, 45% from Carb)
Total Fat 14 g
Saturated Fat 8 g
Mono Fat 4 g
Cholesterol 108 mg
Sodium 351 mg
Total Carbohydrate 29 g
Dietary Fiber 1 g
Sugars 16 g
Protein 4 g
Calcium 36 mg
Iron 1 mg

Pandan Chiffon Cake

8 egg whites
½ tsp. cream of tartar
¾ cup sugar
½ cup cake flour
½ cup white whole-wheat flour
1½ tsp. baking powder
½ tsp. salt
⅓ cup canola oil
1 cup coconut milk
6 egg yolks
Pandan extract

With electric mixer, beat egg whites with cream of tartar until stiff. Gradually add half the sugar.

In separate bowl, mix flours, baking powder, salt, and remaining sugar. Add oil, coconut milk, egg yolks, and a few drops pandan extract.

Gently fold egg white and flour mixtures together until well combined.

Pour into an ungreased 10-in. or 12-cup tube pan. Bake 45 min. at 375 degrees, or until toothpick inserted in center comes out clean. Invert but cool completely before removing from pan. Then keep cake refrigerated, due to the coconut milk. Yield: 16 servings.

Note: Pandan extract can be purchased at Asian grocery stores or online. Leaves of the pandan tree have a unique, sweet, almost floral flavor with a touch of citrus, and their extract is popular in Southeast Asian desserts, adding a bright green color.

Nutrition Facts	
Amount Per Serving	
Calories 162 (51% from Fat, 10% from Protein, 40% from Carb)	
Total Fat 9 g	
Saturated Fat 4 g	
Mono Fat 4 g	
Cholesterol 77 mg	
Sodium 152 mg	
Total Carbohydrate 16 g	
Dietary Fiber 1 g	
Sugars 10 g	
Protein 4 g	
Calcium 39 mg	
Iron 1 mg	

Orange Chiffon Cake

CAKE:

8 large eggs, separated

1 cup sugar

1 tsp. orange zest

½ cup orange juice

½ cup cake flour

½ cup whole-wheat pastry flour

1 tsp. cream of tartar

½ tsp. salt

GLAZE:

1 cup powdered sugar

4 tsp. orange juice

1 tsp. orange zest, optional

Nutrition Facts	
Amount Per Serving of Cake	
Calories 129 (21% from Fat, 14% from Protein, 65% from Carb)	
Total Fat 3 g	
Saturated Fat 1 g	
Mono Fat 1 g	
Cholesterol 123 mg	
Sodium 115 mg	
Total Carbohydrate 21 g	
Dietary Fiber 1 g	
Sugars 13 g	
Protein 5 g	
Calcium 19 mg	
Iron 1 mg	

For cake, with electric mixer, beat egg yolks until frothy. Gradually add ½ cup sugar, continuing to beat until thick.

In small bowl, combine orange zest and juice. Add to yolk mixture alternately with the flours, beating until well blended.

Wash and dry beaters. In another bowl, combine egg whites, cream of tartar, and salt. Beat until soft peaks form. Gradually add remaining sugar. Beat until stiff peaks form. Gently fold egg whites into yolk mixture.

Pour batter into an ungreased 10-in. or 12-cup tube pan. Bake approximately 1 hour and 10 min. in a preheated 325-degree oven, until toothpick inserted in center comes out clean. Cool 10 min., then invert onto a wire rack to cool completely.

Whisk glaze ingredients together and drizzle over cake. Let cake sit approximately 20 min., until glaze is set. Yield: 16 servings.

Nutrition Facts	
Amount Per Recipe of Glaze	
Calories 476 (0% from Fat, 0% from Protein, 100% from Carb)	
Total Fat 0 g	
Saturated Fat 0 g	
Mono Fat 0 g	
Cholesterol 0 mg	
Sodium 1 mg	
Total Carbohydrate 122 g	
Dietary Fiber 0 g	
Sugars 117 g	
Protein 0 g	
Calcium 3 mg	
Iron 0 mg	

Orange Flower Bundt Cake

CAKE:
½ cup butter, softened
½ cup trans-fat-free shortening
1¼ cups sugar
1¼ cups Splenda®
5 eggs, well beaten
1½ cups cake flour
1½ cups white whole-wheat flour
½ tsp. baking powder
1 cup milk
1 tbsp. orange extract
1 tbsp. vanilla extract

GLAZE:
1 cup Splenda®
½ cup water
1 tbsp. orange extract
1 tbsp. vanilla extract

For cake, in large bowl with electric mixer, cream butter, shortening, sugar, and Splenda®. Add eggs and mix well.

Sift together flours and baking powder. Add flour mixture, alternately in small amounts with milk, to butter mixture. Stir in extracts.

Pour batter into a well-greased and -floured 10-in. or 12-cup Bundt pan. Bake 1½ hours in a preheated 325-degree oven, or until toothpick inserted in center comes out clean. Cool 10 min. before removing from pan. Frost with glaze while cake is still warm.

For glaze, mix ingredients together in small, heavy saucepan. Bring to a boil over medium heat. Reduce and simmer until glaze has thickened, approximately 5 min.

Brush ¼ of the glaze onto bottom of warm cake with a pastry brush. Brush remaining glaze over top and sides of cake. Let cool to room temperature before serving. Yield: 16 servings.

Note: Many Middle Eastern desserts use orange flower water,

made from bitter orange blossoms. It is hard to obtain in the U.S., so I use orange extract in this traditional cake.

Nutrition Facts	
Amount Per Serving of Cake	
Calories 292 (44% from Fat, 7% from Protein, 49% from Carb)	
Total Fat 15 g	
Saturated Fat 6 g	
Mono Fat 5 g	
Cholesterol 93 mg	
Sodium 85 mg	
Total Carbohydrate 36 g	
Dietary Fiber 2 g	
Sugars 16 g	
Protein 5 g	
Calcium 34 mg	
Iron 2 mg	

Nutrition Facts	
Amount Per Recipe of Glaze	
Calories 96 (0% from Fat, 0% from Protein, 100% from Carb)	
Total Fat 0 g	
Saturated Fat 0 g	
Mono Fat 0 g	
Cholesterol 0 mg	
Sodium 2 mg	
Total Carbohydrate 24 g	
Dietary Fiber 0 g	
Sugars 0 g	
Protein 0 g	
Calcium 2 mg	
Iron 0 mg	

Apple Bundt Cake

1½ cups whole-wheat pastry flour
1½ cups white flour
1 tbsp. cinnamon
1 tsp. baking soda
1 tsp. salt
1⅓ cups canola oil
1 cup Splenda®
1 cup sugar
3 eggs
3 cup Granny Smith apples, peeled and chopped
1 cup walnut halves
1 tsp. vanilla extract

Sift together flours, cinnamon, baking soda, and salt. Set aside.

In electric mixer bowl with paddle attachment, combine oil, Splenda®, sugar, and eggs at high speed until lemon colored.

Add flour mixture, just until incorporated.

Add apples, nuts, and vanilla. Dough will be a bit stiff.

Pour batter into a greased 10-in. or 12-cup Bundt pan. Bake 80-90 min. in a preheated 350-degree oven, or until toothpick inserted in center comes out clean. Cool 10 min. before unmolding from pan. Serve with warm, sugar-free caramel sauce, if desired. Yield: 16 servings.

Nutrition Facts

Amount Per Recipe of Glaze

Calories 391 (54% from Fat, 6% from Protein, 40% from Carb)

Total Fat 24 g	
Saturated Fat 2 g	
Mono Fat 12 g	
Cholesterol 46 mg	
Sodium 242 mg	
Total Carbohydrate 40 g	
Dietary Fiber 3 g	
Sugars 15 g	
Protein 6 g	
Calcium 24 mg	
Iron 2 mg	

Sour Cream Pound Cake

1½ cups whole-wheat pastry flour

1½ cups bread flour

1 tsp. baking powder

1¼ cups sugar

1¼ cups Splenda®

1 cup Canola Butter (see index) or Smart Balance® regular spread

6 eggs

½ pt. light sour cream

1½ tsp. vanilla extract

Sift together flours and baking powder and set aside.

In mixing bowl with mixer, beat together sugar, Splenda®, and butter until fluffy. Add eggs 1 at a time, beating 1 min. after each addition. Add sour cream and vanilla, and mix until combined. Add flours and beat 1 min. more.

Pour into greased 10-in. or 12-cup tube or Bundt pan. Bake 1 hour in a preheated 350-degree oven. Cool in pan 10 min. Unmold and cool completely on wire rack. Yield: 16 servings.

Nutrition Facts

Amount Per Serving

Calories 330 (45% from Fat, 8% from Protein, 47% from Carb)

Total Fat 17 g	
Saturated Fat 7 g	
Mono Fat 6 g	
Cholesterol 118 mg	
Sodium 122 mg	
Total Carbohydrate 40 g	
Dietary Fiber 2 g	
Sugars 16 g	
Protein 6 g	
Calcium 54 mg	
Iron 2 mg	

Key Lime Cream Cheese Pound Cake

POUND CAKE:

1¾ cups cake flour

1½ cups white whole-wheat flour

¼ tsp. baking soda

¼. tsp salt

2¼ sticks butter, softened

8 oz. regular or light cream cheese, softened

1½ cups Splenda®

1½ cups sugar

6 large eggs

1 tsp. vanilla extract

3 tbsp. Key lime juice

2 tsp. fine lime zest

Nutrition Facts	
Amount Per Serving of Cake	
Calories 368 (47% from Fat, 8% from Protein, 46% from Carb)	
Total Fat 19 g	
Saturated Fat 11 g	
Mono Fat 5 g	
Cholesterol 138 mg	
Sodium 232 mg	
Total Carbohydrate 42 g	
Dietary Fiber 2 g	
Sugars 19 g	
Protein 7 g	
Calcium 38 mg	
Iron 2 mg	

GLAZE:

¼ cup Key lime juice

¾ cup Splenda®

Sift together flours, baking soda, and salt; set aside.

With electric mixer, beat butter and cream cheese at medium speed until creamy and smooth, approximately 4 min. Add Splenda® and sugar and continue beating until light and fluffy, approximately 5 min., stopping to scrape sides and bottom of bowl occasionally. Add eggs 1 at a time, beating well after each. Beat in vanilla and lime juice.

Reduce speed to low and add in flour mixture in 3 additions, mixing just until smooth. Fold in zest.

Spoon batter into a greased and floured 9- or 10-in. or 12-cup Bundt or tube pan, making the sides higher than the center. Bake approximately 1½ hours in a preheated 325-degree oven, or until cake is golden and toothpick inserted in center comes out clean.

Nutrition Facts	
Amount Per Recipe of Glaze	
Calories 89 (1% from Fat, 1% from Protein, 98% from Carb)	
Total Fat 0 g	
Saturated Fat 0 g	
Mono Fat 0 g	
Cholesterol 0 mg	
Sodium 1 mg	
Total Carbohydrate 24 g	
Dietary Fiber 0 g	
Sugars 1 g	
Protein 0 g	
Calcium 6 mg	
Iron 0 mg	

Cool 10 min. before unmolding from pan. Cool completely on wire rack before glazing.

Whisk together glaze ingredients. Glaze cake and let sit 10 min. Sprinkle lightly with powdered sugar, if desired. Yield: 16 servings.

Mango Cream Cheese Pound Cake

1½ cups butter, softened
1 (8-oz.) pkg. light cream cheese, softened
1¼ cups sugar
1¼ cups Splenda®
1 tsp. vanilla extract
1 tsp. orange extract
1 tsp. lemon extract
1½ cups cake flour
1½ cups whole-wheat pastry flour, divided
6 eggs
2 cups diced ripe mangos

Cream together butter, cream cheese, sugar, and Splenda® until light and fluffy. Add extracts. Mix cake flour and 1¼ cups pastry flour. Add alternately with eggs to butter mixture, beginning and ending with flour. Mix remaining ¼ cup pastry flour with mangos. Gently fold into batter.

Pour batter into a greased 12-in. tube or Bundt pan. Bake 1 hour and 20 min. in a preheated 325-degree oven, or until toothpick inserted in center comes out clean. Let cool in pan 10 min. before unmolding. Cool completely on wire rack. If desired, dust with powdered sugar or add a light glaze. Yield: 16 servings.

Note: Peaches may be substituted for the mangos in this recipe.

Nutrition Facts	
Amount Per Serving	
Calories 400 Cal (49% from Fat, 7% from Protein, 43% from Carb)	
Total Fat 22 g	
Saturated Fat 13 g	
Mono Fat 6 g	
Cholesterol 146 mg	
Sodium 196 mg	
Total Carbohydrate 44 g	
Dietary Fiber 3 g	
Sugars 19 g	
Protein 7 g	
Calcium 42 mg	
Iron 2 mg	

Pineapple Rum Pound Cake

POUND CAKE:

3 sticks butter

1 cup Splenda®

1 cup brown sugar

6 eggs

1½ cups whole-wheat pastry flour

1½ cups bread flour

1 tsp. baking powder

¼ cup milk

1 tsp. vanilla extract

¾ cup crushed pineapple, undrained

Plain or toasted coconut

RUM GLAZE:

1 cup butter

½ cup sugar

½ cup Splenda®

½ cup rum

Nutrition Facts		
Amount Per Serving of Cake		
Calories 352 (51% from Fat, 7% from Protein, 43% from Carb)		
Total Fat 20 g		
Saturated Fat 12 g		
Mono Fat 5 g		
Cholesterol 138 mg		
Sodium 192 mg		
Total Carbohydrate 38 g		
Dietary Fiber 2 g		
Sugars 15g		
Protein 6 g		
Calcium 55 mg		
Iron 2 mg		

Cream together butter, Splenda®, and brown sugar. Add eggs 1 at a time, beating 1 min. after each addition. Sift together flours and baking powder. Add alternately with milk to creamed mixture, a little at a time. Add vanilla and undrained pineapple, and blend well.

Pour batter into a greased and floured 10-in. or 12-cup tube or Bundt pan. Place in cold oven and turn oven to 325 degrees. Bake ½ hour or until toothpick inserted in center comes out clean.

Let cake cool in pan 10 min. Run knife around edges to loosen and carefully invert. Cool completely on wire rack before glazing.

For glaze, melt butter over low heat. Add sugar and Splenda®, stirring until dissolved. Remove from heat and add rum.

Nutrition Facts		
Amount Per Recipe of Glaze		
Calories 2,323 (78% from Fat, 0% from Protein, 21% from Carb)		
Total Fat 184 g		
Saturated Fat 117 g		
Mono Fat 48 g		
Cholesterol 488 mg		
Sodium 1,309 mg		
Total Carbohydrate 113 g		
Dietary Fiber 0 g		
Sugars 101 g		
Protein 2 g		
Calcium 55 mg		
Iron 0 mg		

Prick top of cake with fork all over. Pour glaze over and let fall down sides of cake. Top with coconut. Yield: 16 servings.

Note: This cake also works well with half white flour and half white whole-wheat flour.

Maraschino Cherry Pound Cake

1¼ cups whole-wheat pastry flour, divided
1 cup bread flour
1 tbsp. baking powder
½ tsp. salt
1 cup butter
1 (8-oz) pkg. light cream cheese
¾ cup sugar
¾ cup Splenda®
4 eggs
1 tsp. vanilla extract
1 tsp. almond extract
1 cup or more maraschino cherries, drained and halved
Powdered sugar

Mix together 1 cup whole-wheat pastry flour, the bread flour, baking powder, and salt; set aside.

Cream together butter, cream cheese, sugar, and Splenda® until light and fluffy. Beat in eggs 1 at a time. Stir in vanilla and almond extracts. Beat in flour mixture just until incorporated.

Dredge cherries in remaining flour and fold into batter.

Pour into a greased and floured 8-in. tube or Bundt pan. Bake 60-80 min. at 325 degrees, or until toothpick inserted in center comes out clean. Cool 10 min. before unmolding. Cool completely on wire rack. Dust with powdered sugar. Yield: 16 servings.

Nutrition Facts	
Amount Per Serving	
Calories 283 (48% from Fat, 8% from Protein, 44% from Carb)	
Total Fat 16 g	
Saturated Fat 9 g	
Mono Fat 4 g	
Cholesterol 100 mg	
Sodium 310 mg	
Total Carbohydrate 33 g	
Dietary Fiber 2 g	
Sugars 11 g	
Protein 6 g	
Calcium 84 mg	
Iron 2 mg	

7Up® Pound Cake

3 sticks butter, softened
1¼ cups sugar
1¼ cups Splenda®
5 eggs
1 tsp. lemon extract
1 tsp. vanilla extract
1½ cups cake flour
1½ cups white whole-wheat flour
1 cup Diet 7Up® soda

Cream butter with sugar and Splenda® until fluffy. Add eggs 1 at a time, beating 1 min. after each addition. Add extracts. Add flours and soda alternately, beating well after each addition.

Pour into a greased and floured large tube or Bundt pan. Bake 1½ hours in a 300-degree oven, or until toothpick inserted in center comes out clean. Cool in pan 10 min. Unmold and cool completely on wire rack. Yield: 16 servings.

Note: You may prefer to use 1½ cups whole-wheat pastry flour and 1½ cups bread flour in this recipe.

Nutrition Facts

Amount Per Serving

Calories 333 (52% from Fat, 6% from Protein, 43% from Carb)

Total Fat 19 g	
Saturated Fat 12 g	
Mono Fat 5 g	
Cholesterol 122 mg	
Sodium 149 mg	
Total Carbohydrate 36 g	
Dietary Fiber 2 g	
Sugars 16 g	
Protein 5 g	
Calcium 21 mg	
Iron 2 mg	

Plantation Pound Cake

1 cup cake flour
¾ cup white whole-wheat flour
1 tsp. lemon zest
¾ tsp. baking soda
½ tsp. salt
½ cup butter or Smart Balance® regular spread, softened
1 cup sugar
4 eggs
½ cup light or regular sour cream
1 tsp. lemon juice
1 tsp. vanilla extract
1 cup ground almonds, walnuts, or pecans
Powdered sugar for dusting

Stir together flours, zest, baking soda, and salt; set aside.

In large mixing bowl with electric mixer, beat together butter and sugar at medium speed until light and fluffy. Beat in eggs, sour cream, lemon juice, and vanilla until thoroughly blended. Switch mixer to low speed and beat in flour mixture, ½ cup at a time, just until blended.

Pour half of the mixture into a greased and floured 5x9-in. loaf pan. Sprinkle with ground nuts. Top with remaining batter. With a narrow spatula, gently swirl through batter to marble.

Bake 60-70 min. in a preheated 325-degree oven, or until toothpick inserted in center comes out clean. Cool 10 min., remove from pan, and cool completely. Dust with powdered sugar. Yield: 16 servings.

Note: ½ cup sugar and ½ cup Splenda® can be used in place of 1 cup sugar.

Nutrition Facts		
Amount Per Serving		
Calories 235 (48% from Fat, 9% from Protein, 43% from Carb)		
Total Fat 13 g		
Saturated Fat 5 g		
Mono Fat 5 g		
Cholesterol 80 mg		
Sodium 200 mg		
Total Carbohydrate 26 g		
Dietary Fiber 2 g		
Sugars 13 g		
Protein 6 g		
Calcium 40 mg		
Iron 1 mg		

Almond Flour Pound Cake

½ cup butter, softened
½ cup cream cheese, softened
¾ cup sugar
2 tbsp. brown sugar
4 eggs
1 tsp. vanilla or almond extract
2 cups almond flour
1 tsp. baking powder
½ tsp. salt
¼ tsp. ginger
¼ tsp. cardamom
¼ cup slivered almonds
Whipped cream
Berries

In mixing bowl with electric mixer, beat together butter, cream cheese, and sugars until well blended.

Add eggs 1 at a time, beating well after each. Beat in extract.

In medium bowl, combine almond flour, baking powder, salt, ginger, and cardamom. Gradually add dry ingredients to egg mixture on medium speed.

Pour batter into a greased 5x9-in. loaf pan. Sprinkle top with almonds. Bake 45-55 min. in a preheated 350-degree oven, or until toothpick inserted in center comes out clean.

Cool in pan 10 min. before removing from pan. Cool completely on a wire rack. Serve with whipped cream and berries. Yield: 16 servings.

Nutrition Facts

Amount Per Serving

Calories 247 (66% from Fat, 10% from Protein, 24% from Carb)

Total Fat 19 g
  Saturated Fat 6 g
  Mono Fat 9 g
Cholesterol 85 mg
Sodium 193 mg
Total Carbohydrate 15 g
  Dietary Fiber 2 g
  Sugars 12 g
Protein 6 g
Calcium 73 mg
Iron 1 mg

Marbled Angel Food Cake

½ cup cake flour
½ cup whole-wheat pastry flour
Pinch nutmeg
12 egg whites (1¾ cups)
1½ tsp. cream of tartar
1 cup superfine sugar*
¼ cup unsweetened cocoa powder
Strawberries

In medium bowl, sift together flours and nutmeg.

With mixer on medium speed, beat together egg whites and cream of tartar. Beat in sugar, 2 tbsp. at a time. Continue beating 5-7 min., until stiff, glossy peaks form.

Fold flour mixture into egg mixture in 2 additions until incorporated. Transfer half of the batter to a medium bowl and gently fold in cocoa powder.

Spoon the light batter alternately with the chocolate batter into an ungreased 10-in. tube pan. Swirl a sharp knife through the batter to create a marbled effect.

Bake 40 min. in a preheated 350-degree oven, or until cake springs back when touched and toothpick inserted in center comes out clean. Invert pan onto wire rack and cool 1 hour before removing cake onto a serving plate. Serve with strawberries. Yield: 16 servings.

*To make superfine sugar, pulse regular sugar in blender or food processor until superfine.

Nutrition Facts

Amount Per Serving

Calories 99 (3% from Fat, 15% from Protein, 82% from Carb)

Total Fat 0 g	
Saturated Fat 0 g	
Mono Fat 0 g	
Cholesterol 0 mg	
Sodium 42 mg	
Total Carbohydrate 21 g	
Dietary Fiber 1 g	
Sugars 13 g	
Protein 4 g	
Calcium 6 mg	
Iron 1 mg	

Self-Frosting Angel Food Cake

6 egg whites, room temperature
½ tsp. cream of tartar
⅛ tsp. salt
¼ cup sugar
2 tbsp. Splenda®
½ cup cake flour, sifted
½ tsp. vanilla extract
⅛ tsp. almond extract
½ cup flaked coconut

With electric mixer, beat egg whites until foamy. Add cream of tartar and salt, and beat until soft peaks form. Gradually add sugar and Splenda®, 2 tbsp. at a time, beating mixture until stiff peaks form.

Sprinkle flour over egg white mixture; fold in carefully. Gently fold in extracts.

Pour batter into an ungreased 9-in. square baking pan. Sprinkle coconut over top. Bake 30 min. in a preheated 350-degree oven, or until toothpick inserted in center comes out clean. Cool in pan approximately 40 min. before removing. Cut into squares to serve. Yield: 9 servings.

Nutrition Facts

Amount Per Serving

Calories 82 (16% from Fat, 16% from Protein, 68% from Carb)

Total Fat 1 g	
Saturated Fat 1 g	
Mono Fat 0 g	
Cholesterol 0 mg	
Sodium 71 mg	
Total Carbohydrate 14 g	
Dietary Fiber 0 g	
Sugars 6 g	
Protein 3 g	
Calcium 3 mg	
Iron 1 mg	

Punch Bowl Cake

1 angel food cake
1 (1.5-oz.) box sugar-free instant vanilla pudding mix
2 cups milk
1 (20-oz.) can crushed pineapple, drained
1 (20-oz.) can light cherry or strawberry pie filling
8 oz. frozen whipped topping, thawed
½ cup pecans, chopped
Maraschino cherries

Cut the angel food cake in half crosswise. Mix pudding with milk per pkg. directions. In large glass bowl or trifle bowl, layer cake in following order, making 2 layers:

cake
pineapple
pie filling
pudding
whipped topping

Garnish top with pecans and cherries. Chill at least 2 hours. Recipe can be doubled for large crowds. Yield: 16 servings.

Nutrition Facts	
Amount Per Serving	
Calories 126 (46% from Fat, 5% from Protein, 49% from Carb)	
Total Fat 7 g	
Saturated Fat 4 g	
Mono Fat 2 g	
Cholesterol 2 mg	
Sodium 138 mg	
Total Carbohydrate 16 g	
Dietary Fiber 1 g	
Sugars 12 g	
Protein 2 g	
Calcium 36 mg	
Iron 0 mg	

Two-Ingredient Cakes

A post on a homemaking forum I belong to reminded me about the 2-ingredient cake-mix desserts. I was first introduced to these recipes through Weight Watchers®. These are great for diabetics because they omit the eggs and oil that are typically needed to bake a cake. Try the new reduced-sugar cake mixes from Pillsbury® in these recipes and you'll really do your body a favor. These recipes work well for low-carbers and non-diabetics also, so feel free to serve these to your friends or whole family.

Pineapple Angel Food Cake

1 (18.25-oz.) pkg. angel food cake mix, reduced sugar
1 (20-oz.) can crushed pineapple, undrained

Mix ingredients well with large spoon. Do not add anything else. Follow pkg. directions for baking. This is great topped with whipped cream or frozen whipped topping. Yield: 16 servings.

Nutrition Facts	
Amount Per Serving	
Calories 139 (1% from Fat, 8% from Protein, 90% from Carb)	
Total Fat 0 g	
Saturated Fat 0 g	
Mono Fat 0 g	
Cholesterol 0 mg	
Sodium 239 mg	
Total Carbohydrate 32 g	
Dietary Fiber 0 g	
Sugars 19 g	
Protein 3 g	
Calcium 44 mg	
Iron 0 mg	

Devil's Food Cake

1 (18.25-oz.) pkg. devil's food cake mix, reduced sugar
10 oz. diet cola or diet root beer

Mix ingredients well and pour into a 9x13-in. baking pan that has been greased and dusted with cocoa powder. Bake according to pkg. directions at 350 degrees. Cake will be a bit denser than regular chocolate cake—more similar to a cake brownie. Yield: 16 servings.

VARIATION:

Try with reduced-sugar white or yellow cake mix and diet Sprite®.

Nutrition Facts

Amount Per Serving

Calories 138 (31% from Fat, 5% from Protein, 64% from Carb)

Total Fat 5 g	
Saturated Fat 1 g	
Mono Fat 2 g	
Cholesterol 0 mg	
Sodium 267 mg	
Total Carbohydrate 24 g	
Dietary Fiber 1 g	
Sugars 12 g	
Protein 2 g	
Calcium 49 mg	
Iron 1 mg	

Chocolate Cherry Cake

1 (18.25-oz.) pkg. chocolate cake mix, regular or reduced sugar
2 eggs
1 (20-oz.) can light cherry pie filling

Mix together all ingredients and bake according to pkg. directions. No need to frost. Yield: 16 servings.

Nutrition Facts

Amount Per Serving

Calories 165 (30% from Fat, 7% from Protein, 63% from Carb)

Total Fat 6 g	
Saturated Fat 1 g	
Mono Fat 2 g	
Cholesterol 31 mg	
Sodium 281 mg	
Total Carbohydrate 27 g	
Dietary Fiber 1 g	
Sugars 16 g	
Protein 3 g	
Calcium 56 mg	
Iron 2 mg	

Boston Cream Pie

1 (18.25-oz.) pkg. yellow cake mix, regular or reduced sugar
1 (2.1-oz) pkg. sugar-free instant vanilla pudding mix
1 (15-oz.) can reduced-sugar chocolate frosting

Prepare cake batter according to pkg. directions. Bake in 2 round pans. Cool and remove from pans.

While cake is baking, make pudding according to pkg. directions and refrigerate. For a thicker pudding, use a bit less milk than pkg. calls for.

Spread pudding over bottom layer of cake, leaving approximately 1 in. of the edges clean. Place second cake layer on top.

Open frosting container and peel off foil. Re-cover with lid and microwave in 20-second intervals, stirring between intervals until frosting can be poured but is not boiling (about the consistency of thick syrup). Let cool a few minutes. Spoon over top of cake, until top is covered and frosting runs down sides of cake. Place 1 maraschino cherry in center, if desired. Keep refrigerated. Yield: 16 servings.

Nutrition Facts		
Amount Per Serving		
Calories 314 (40% from Fat, 4% from Protein, 56% from Carb)		
Total Fat 14 g		
Saturated Fat 3 g		
Mono Fat 7 g		
Cholesterol 47 mg		
Sodium 431 mg		
Total Carbohydrate 45 g		
Dietary Fiber 1 g		
Sugars 29 g		
Protein 3 g		
Calcium 57 mg		
Iron 1 mg		

Lemon Meringue Cake

CAKE:

1 (18.25-oz.) pkg. yellow cake mix, regular or reduced sugar

FILLING:

1 cup Splenda®

3 tbsp. cornstarch

¼ tsp. salt

½ cup water

¼ cup lemon juice

4 egg yolks, beaten

4 tsp. butter

1 tsp. lemon zest

MERINGUE:

4 egg whites

¼ tsp. cream of tartar

¾ cup Splenda®

For cake, prepare cake mix according to pkg. directions and pour batter into a greased 9x13-in. baking pan. Bake according to pkg. directions and cool.

For filling, combine Splenda®, corn-starch, and salt in saucepan. Stir in water and lemon juice until smooth. Bring to a boil. Cook and stir 1-2 min., or until thick.

Remove from heat and stir small amount of hot mixture into egg yolks. Return to pan, stirring constantly, until mixture comes to a gentle boil. Cook and continue stirring 2 min. Remove from heat. Stir in butter and lemon zest. Cool completely and spread filling over top of cooled cake.

For meringue, in mixing bowl, beat egg whites and cream of tartar until foamy. On high speed, gradually beat in Splenda® until

Nutrition Facts		
Amount Per Serving		
Calories 185 (28% from Fat, 7% from Protein, 65% from Carb)		
Total Fat 6 g		
Saturated Fat 2 g		
Mono Fat 2 g		
Cholesterol 54 mg		
Sodium 275 mg		
Total Carbohydrate 30 g		
Dietary Fiber 0 g		
Sugars 14 g		
Protein 3 g		
Calcium 51 mg		
Iron 1 mg		

stiff peaks form. Spread meringue over lemon filling, sealing edges. Bake 10-15 min. in a preheated 350-degree oven, or until meringue is lightly browned. Cake can be served warm or chilled. Yield: 16 servings.

Italian Love Cake

1 (18.25-oz.) pkg. chocolate cake mix, regular or reduced sugar
2 lb. ricotta cheese
1 cup Splenda®
4 eggs
1 tsp. vanilla extract
1 (2.1-oz) box sugar-free instant chocolate pudding mix
1 cup milk
8 oz. nondairy frozen whipped topping, thawed
Maraschino cherries for garnish

Prepare cake mix according to pkg. directions and spread into a greased and floured 9x13-in. baking pan.

In separate bowl, combine ricotta, Splenda®, eggs, and vanilla, and mix well. Spoon mixture over cake batter in pan. Bake 1 hour in a preheated 350-degree oven. Cool completely.

Mix pudding mix with milk, and fold in whipped topping. Spread over cooled cake. Garnish with cherries.

Refrigerate until ready to serve. Yield: 16 servings.

Nutrition Facts	
Amount Per Serving	
Calories 306 (42% from Fat, 14% from Protein, 44% from Carb)	
Total Fat 15 g	
Saturated Fat 8 g	
Mono Fat 4 g	
Cholesterol 80 mg	
Sodium 472 mg	
Total Carbohydrate 35 g	
Dietary Fiber 1 g	
Sugars 16 g	
Protein 11 g	
Calcium 225 mg	
Iron 2 mg	

Sunshine Cake

CAKE:

1 (11-oz.) can mandarin oranges with juice
Water
1 (18.25-oz). pkg. yellow cake mix, regular or reduced sugar
2 eggs

TOPPING:

16 oz. frozen whipped topping, thawed
1 (20-oz.) can crushed pineapple, drained
1 pkg. sugar-free instant vanilla pudding mix

Drain oranges, reserving juice. Add enough water to the juice to equal 1⅓ cups liquid. Mix together cake mix, eggs, and liquid. Add oranges and mix.

Pour into a greased 9x13-in. baking pan. Bake 30-35 min. in a preheated 350-degree oven. Remove from pan and cool completely on wire rack.

Mix topping ingredients together. Add to top of cake. Yield: 16 servings.

Nutrition Facts	
Amount Per Serving	
Calories 272 (38% from Fat, 4% from Protein, 58% from Carb)	
Total Fat 12 g	
Saturated Fat 7 g	
Mono Fat 2 g	
Cholesterol 31 mg	
Sodium 264 mg	
Total Carbohydrate 40 g	
Dietary Fiber 1 g	
Sugars 27 g	
Protein 3 g	
Calcium 57 mg	
Iron 1 mg	

Dreamsicle Cake

1 (18.25-oz.) pkg. yellow cake mix, regular or reduced sugar
2 eggs
1 (12-oz.) can sugar-free orange soda
2 (.3-oz.) pkg. sugar-free orange Jell-O®
1 cup boiling water
1 cup cold water
1 (1.5-oz.) pkg. sugar-free vanilla pudding mix
1 cup milk
1 tsp. vanilla extract
8 oz. frozen whipped topping, thawed

Mix together cake mix, eggs, and orange soda. Pour batter into a greased 9x13-in. baking pan.

Bake 20-30 min. in a preheated 350-degree oven, or until toothpick inserted in center comes out clean.

Remove cake from oven. Poke holes in cake with a fork sprayed with cooking spray.

Mix 1 pkg. Jell-O® with the boiling water and stir until dissolved. Add the cold water. Pour mixture over cake. Refrigerate at least 2 hours.

Mix together pudding mix and remaining Jell-O®. Add milk and vanilla extract. Mix well. Blend in whipped topping, and frost cake. Keep cake refrigerated. Yield: 16 servings.

Nutrition Facts

Amount Per Serving

Calories 227 (34% from Fat, 10% from Protein, 56% from Carb)

Total Fat 8 g	
Saturated Fat 4 g	
Mono Fat 2 g	
Cholesterol 32 mg	
Sodium 462 mg	
Total Carbohydrate 31 g	
Dietary Fiber 0 g	
Sugars 18 g	
Protein 6 g	
Calcium 62 mg	
Iron 1 mg	

Jell-O® Poke Cake

CAKE:

1 (18.25-oz.) pkg. white cake mix
1 (.3-oz.) pkg. sugar-free Jell-O®, any flavor
¾ cup boiling water

TOPPING:

1 pkg. sugar-free instant vanilla pudding mix
2½ cups milk
1 tsp. vanilla extract
4 oz. frozen whipped topping, thawed

Prepare cake according to pkg. directions. Bake in a 9x13-in. baking pan as directed. Cool 25 min.

Dissolve Jell-O® in boiling water. Poke holes in cooled cake with a fork, spacing holes about ½ in. apart. Slowly pour dissolved Jell-O® into holes.

Mix together all topping ingredients and spread over cake. Refrigerate. Yield: 16 servings.

Nutrition Facts

Amount Per Serving

Calories 209 (34% from Fat, 11% from Protein, 55% from Carb)

Total Fat 8 g	
Saturated Fat 3 g	
Mono Fat 3 g	
Cholesterol 2 mg	
Sodium 356 mg	
Total Carbohydrate 28 g	
Dietary Fiber 0 g	
Sugars 20 g	
Protein 6 g	
Calcium 86 mg	
Iron 1 mg	

Dump Cake

1 (20-oz.) can crushed pineapple in syrup
1 (20-oz.) can light cherry pie filling
1 (18.25-oz.) pkg. yellow cake mix, regular or reduced sugar
¾ stick butter
1 cup pecans, chopped

Layer first 3 ingredients in order listed in a greased 9x13-in. baking pan. (The cake mix will be a dry layer.) Dot with butter and sprinkle with pecans. Bake 1 hour at 350 degrees. Serve with whipped cream or whipped topping, if desired. Yield: 16 servings.

Note: This also works well with 2 cans pitted dark Bing cherries in heavy syrup, in place of 1 can cherry pie filling. Drain 1 can Bing cherries and proceed as above.

Nutrition Facts		
Amount Per Serving		
Calories 262 (44% from Fat, 4% from Protein, 52% from Carb)		
Total Fat 13 g		
Saturated Fat 4 g		
Mono Fat 6 g		
Cholesterol 12 mg		
Sodium 250 mg		
Total Carbohydrate 35 g		
Dietary Fiber 2 g		
Sugars 8 g		
Protein 3 g		
Calcium 59 mg		
Iron 1 mg		

Pineapple Upside-Down Cake

1 (18.25-oz.) pkg. yellow cake mix, regular or reduced sugar
¼ cup butter or Smart Balance® regular spread
½ cup brown sugar or Splenda® Brown Sugar Blend
1 (20-oz.) can no-sugar-added pineapple rings
Maraschino cherries

Prepare cake batter according to pkg. directions and set aside.

Melt butter or spread in 12-in. cast-iron skillet. Sprinkle in brown sugar or brown sugar blend evenly. Arrange pineapple slices evenly in pan and place 1 cherry inside each pineapple ring.

Spread cake batter over pineapples. Bake approximately 35 min. at 350 degrees, or until toothpick inserted in center comes out clean. Cool 2 min. and invert onto serving plate. Serve with whipped cream or whipped topping, if desired. Yield: 12 servings.

Nutrition Facts

Amount Per Serving

Calories 385 (45% from Fat, 4% from Protein, 51% from Carb)

Total Fat 19 g	
Saturated Fat 4 g	
Mono Fat 9 g	
Cholesterol 72 mg	
Sodium 335 mg	
Total Carbohydrate 50 g	
Dietary Fiber 1 g	
Sugars 34 g	
Protein 4 g	
Calcium 82 mg	
Iron 1 mg	

Walnut Cream Cake Roll

CAKE:
4 eggs, divided
½ cup sugar
2 tsp. vanilla extract
Pinch salt
¼ cup white or white whole-wheat flour
½ cup walnuts or pecans, chopped
Powdered sugar

FILLING:
1 cup whipping cream
2 tbsp. powdered sugar
2 tsp. vanilla extract

DECORATION:
Chopped walnuts or pecans
Maraschino cherries

With electric mixer, beat egg whites until stiff. Add sugar, vanilla, and salt; set aside.

Beat egg yolks by hand until thick and lemon colored. Fold egg whites into yolks. Fold in flour and nuts just until combined. Do not overmix.

Line a jellyroll pan with parchment or waxed paper. Pour in cake batter and spread to edges. Bake 12 min. in a preheated 375-degree oven. Remove from oven and cool 5 min.

Sprinkle a clean tea towel with powdered sugar, and turn cake out on towel. Peel off paper. Cool slightly. Roll cake with towel, jellyroll fashion. Refrigerate 1 hour.

For filling, whip cream. Add sugar and vanilla and combine.

Unroll cake and spread with most of the filling. Roll into a log and decorate with reserved filling, nuts, and cherries. Yield: 12 servings.

Nutrition Facts
Amount Per Serving
Calories 142 (52% from Fat, 12% from Protein, 37% from Carb)
Total Fat 8 g
Saturated Fat 3 g
Mono Fat 2 g
Cholesterol 93 mg
Sodium 55 mg
Total Carbohydrate 13 g
Dietary Fiber 0 g
Sugars 10 g
Protein 4 g
Calcium 21 mg
Iron 1 mg

Coconut Jellyroll

4 eggs

⅔ cup sugar

¾ cup whole-wheat pastry flour

¾ tsp. baking powder

¼ tsp. salt

1 tsp. vanilla extract

Powdered sugar

1 cup sugar-free or reduced-sugar jelly or jam, room temperature

1 cup sweetened flaked coconut

With electric mixer, beat eggs until light. Gradually add sugar and beat until mixture is thick and lemon colored.

Combine flour, baking powder, and salt. Fold with vanilla into egg mixture. Pour into 15x10-in. jellyroll pan that has been lined with greased parchment paper. Spread to edges.

Bake approximately 15 min. at 400 degrees. Cut edges off cake and turn cake at once onto a clean tea towel sprinkled with powdered sugar.

Remove the paper from cake. Spread cake with jelly or jam to within ½ in. of edges. Sprinkle with coconut. Roll up quickly, starting at narrow side of cake. End with open end on the underside. Wrap in towel and cool on wire rack. Once cooled, wrap in plastic wrap and refrigerate. This is best eaten the next day. Yield: 12 servings.

Nutrition Facts
Amount Per Serving
Calories 172 (23% from Fat, 8% from Protein, 69% from Carb)
Total Fat 5 g
Saturated Fat 3 g
Mono Fat 1 g
Cholesterol 82 mg
Sodium 127 mg
Total Carbohydrate 33 g
Dietary Fiber 2 g
Sugars 22 g
Protein 4 g
Calcium 34 mg
Iron 1 mg

Lemon or Lime Meringue Roulade

ROULADE:

4 egg whites
½ cup sugar
½ cup Splenda®
1 tsp. almond extract
1 tsp. white wine vinegar
¼ cup ground almonds
½ pt. whipping cream
2 tbsp. powdered sugar, sifted
Toasted sliced almonds

LEMON OR LIME CURD:

3 eggs
½ cup sugar
½ cup Splenda®
½ cup fresh lemon or lime juice
¼ cup butter, melted
1 tbsp. lemon or lime zest

Preheat oven to 325 degrees. Line jellyroll pan with a single sheet of parchment paper.

In mixing bowl with mixer, beat egg whites until stiff peaks form. Mix sugar and Splenda®. Gradually beat into egg whites 1 tbsp. at a time. Stir in almond extract, vinegar, and ground almonds and mix together lightly.

Pour batter into the parchment-lined jellyroll pan, smoothing the top with a spatula. Tap pan lightly to remove any air bubbles. Bake 30-35 min. or until top is a pale golden color and feels firm and set. Remove from oven and cool.

In the meantime, whip cream until thick. Set aside.

For lemon or lime curd, beat together eggs, sugar, and Splenda® in the top of a double boiler. Stir in juice, butter, and zest. Cook over simmering water 15 min. or until thickened.

Invert cooled roulade onto a large sheet of parchment paper sprinkled with the 2 tbsp. powdered sugar. Carefully strip off paper.

Spread roulade with 6 tbsp. lemon or lime curd and then the whipped cream. Let sit a few minutes to allow the roulade to soften. Carefully roll. The roulade will crack slightly as you roll, which is normal. Sprinkle top with toasted almonds. Yield: 12 servings.

Nutrition Facts	
Amount Per Serving of Roulade	
Calories 95 (43% from Fat, 9% from Protein, 48% from Carb)	
Total Fat 5 g	
Saturated Fat 2 g	
Mono Fat 2 g	
Cholesterol 11 mg	
Sodium 23 mg	
Total Carbohydrate 12 g	
Dietary Fiber 0 g	
Sugars 10 g	
Protein 2 g	
Calcium 14 mg	
Iron 0 mg	

Nutrition Facts	
Amount Per Serving of Curd	
Calories 95 (49% from Fat, 8% from Protein, 43% from Carb)	
Total Fat 5 g	
Saturated Fat 3 g	
Mono Fat 2 g	
Cholesterol 72 mg	
Sodium 48 mg	
Total Carbohydrate 10 g	
Dietary Fiber 0 g	
Sugars 9 g	
Protein 2 g	
Calcium 10 mg	
Iron 0 mg	

Cream Cheese Cupcakes

FILLING:

8 oz. regular or light cream cheese

⅓ cup Splenda®

1 egg

⅛ tsp. salt

1 cup semi-sweet or sugar-free chocolate chips

CUPCAKES:

¾ cup cake flour

¾ cup white whole-wheat flour

¾ cup sugar

⅓ cup cocoa powder

1 tsp. baking soda

½ tsp. salt

⅓ cup canola oil

1 cup water

1 tbsp. vinegar

1 tsp. vanilla extract

For filling, soften cream cheese slightly in microwave. Combine well with Splenda®, egg, and salt. Stir in chocolate chips.

Combine all cupcake ingredients in order given, and blend well with mixer. Line muffin tins with paper cups and fill cups ⅔ full. Spoon 1 tbsp. filling onto each cupcake.

Bake approximately 20 min. in a preheated 350-degree oven. Cool completely before removing from tins. Can be eaten plain, dusted with powdered sugar, or frosted with a cream cheese frosting. Keep refrigerated. Yield: 12 servings.

Nutrition Facts
Amount Per Serving
Calories 308 (50% from Fat, 6% from Protein, 45% from Carb)
Total Fat 18 g
Saturated Fat 7 g
Mono Fat 7 g
Cholesterol 41 mg
Sodium 293 mg
Total Carbohydrate 36 g
Dietary Fiber 3 g
Sugars 21 g
Protein 5 g
Calcium 29 mg
Iron 2 mg

Nutella® Cupcakes

¾ cup sugar

10 tbsp. butter, Canola Butter (see index), or Smart Balance® regular
   spread

3 eggs

⅓ cup milk

½ tsp. vanilla extract

1 cup cake flour

¾ cup white whole-wheat flour

¼ tsp. salt

2 tsp. baking powder

⅓ cup Nutella®

With mixer, cream sugar and butter or butter substitute 2 min.
until light. Add eggs 1 at a time, and continue mixing. Add milk and
vanilla. Stir in dry ingredients.

Line 12 muffin tins with paper liners. With ice cream scoop, fill
cups ¾ full. Top each with 1½ tsp. Nutella® and swirl with toothpick.
Bake approximately 20 min. in a preheated 325-degree oven. Cool
completely before removing from tins. Yield: 12 servings.

Nutrition Facts	
Amount Per Serving	
Calories 260 (45% from Fat, 7% from Protein, 48% from Carb)	
Total Fat 13 g	
Saturated Fat 7 g	
Mono Fat 3 g	
Cholesterol 87 mg	
Sodium 227 mg	
Total Carbohydrate 32 g	
Dietary Fiber 1 g	
Sugars 13 g	
Protein 4 g	
Calcium 64 mg	
Iron 1 mg	

Creme-Filled Cupcakes

CUPCAKES:

1 (18.25-oz.) pkg. chocolate cake mix, regular or reduced sugar

2 tsp. hot water

¼ tsp. salt

1 (8-oz.) jar sugar-free marshmallow creme

½ cup trans-fat-free shortening

⅓ cup powdered sugar

½ tsp. vanilla extract

GANACHE:

1 cup (6 oz.) semi-sweet or sugar-free chocolate chips

¾ cup whipping cream

Prepare and bake cupcakes according to pkg. directions, using paper-lined muffin cups. Cool cupcakes completely.

In small bowl, combine water and salt until salt is dissolved. Let cool.

In small mixing bowl with electric mixer, beat together marshmallow creme, shortening, sugar, and vanilla on high speed until light and fluffy. Add salt mixture.

Insert a small round pastry tip into a pastry bag (or into a plastic bag with 1 corner cut off). Fill bag with creme filling. Insert tip halfway into center of each cupcake, and fill with a small amount of creme.

For ganache, in heavy saucepan, melt chocolate chips with cream. Cool. Dip cupcake tops into ganache. Chill 20 min. or until set. Store cupcakes in refrigerator. Yield: 24 servings.

Note: Sugar-free marshmallow creme is available through www.amazon.com.

Nutrition Facts	
Amount Per Serving	
Calories 211 (44% from Fat, 3% from Protein, 53% from Carb)	
Total Fat 11 g	
Saturated Fat 4 g	
Mono Fat 4 g	
Cholesterol 4 mg	
Sodium 212 mg	
Total Carbohydrate 30 g	
Dietary Fiber 1 g	
Sugars 19 g	
Protein 2 g	
Calcium 37 mg	
Iron 1 mg	

Amaretto Cheesecake

1 cup crushed graham crackers
3 tbsp. butter, melted
4 (8-oz.) pkg. light cream cheese
Dash salt
1 tsp. vanilla extract
4 eggs
1⅓ cups Splenda®
½ cup amaretto
2 cups light sour cream
½ cup sliced almonds

Combine graham cracker crumbs and butter. Press mixture into bottom and sides of a buttered 10-in. springform pan. Set aside.

Beat together cream cheese, salt, vanilla, eggs, Splenda®, and amaretto. Fold in the sour cream. Pour into crust. Bake 45 min. in a preheated 375-degree oven or until set. During last 10 min. of baking, add almonds evenly to top of cheesecake.

Cool. Store in refrigerator. Yield: 12-16 servings.

Nutrition Facts

Amount Per Serving

Calories 375 (66% from Fat, 15% from Protein, 19% from Carb)

Total Fat 27 g	
Saturated Fat 14 g	
Mono Fat 9 g	
Cholesterol 147 mg	
Sodium 333 mg	
Total Carbohydrate 18 g	
Dietary Fiber 1 g	
Sugars 4 g	
Protein 13 g	
Calcium 153 mg	
Iron 2 mg	

Sour Cream-Topped Cheesecake

CRUST:

11 graham crackers

4 tbsp. butter, melted

½ tsp. sugar

¼ tsp. cinnamon

FILLING:

12 oz. cream cheese, softened

3 eggs

½ cup sugar or Splenda®

1½ tsp. vanilla extract

TOPPING:

½ pt. sour cream

2 tbsp. sugar or Splenda®

½ tsp. vanilla extract

For crust, crush graham crackers. Add butter, sugar, and cinnamon. Press mixture into bottom and sides of a springform pan.

With electric mixer, cream the cream cheese. Add 1 egg along with some sugar. Add another egg along with some sugar. Add last egg with remaining sugar. Add vanilla.

Pour mixture into center of crust and spread out. Bake 45-60 min. in a preheated 325-degree oven or until set. Cool, and keep in pan.

Combine all topping ingredients and spread on top of cooled cheesecake. Bake exactly 5 min. in a preheated 475-degree oven. Remove and chill in refrigerator at least 4 hours before serving. Yield: 12-16 servings.

Nutrition Facts
Amount Per Serving
Calories 284 (60% from Fat, 8% from Protein, 32% from Carb)
Total Fat 19 g
Saturated Fat 11 g
Mono Fat 6 g
Cholesterol 111 mg
Sodium 219 mg
Total Carbohydrate 23 g
Dietary Fiber 0 g
Sugars 15 g
Protein 5 g
Calcium 57 mg
Iron 1 mg

Miniature Cheesecakes

CHEESECAKES:

3 (8-oz.) pkg. cream cheese, softened

1 cup Splenda®

6 eggs

1½ tsp. vanilla extract

1 box vanilla wafers

TOPPING:

1 pt. sour cream

1½ tsp. vanilla extract

½ cup Splenda®

With electric mixer, combine cream cheese and Splenda®. Add eggs, 1 at a time, beating well after each addition. Add vanilla.

Place 1 vanilla wafer in each cavity of a muffin tin. Pour mixture on top of each wafer, filling cups ¾ full. Bake 20-25 min. in a preheated 300-degree oven.

Combine all topping ingredients well.

Immediately add topping to baked cheesecakes, and bake an additional 10 min. Cool and keep refrigerated. Yield: 24 servings.

Nutrition Facts		
Amount Per Serving		
Calories 224 (67% from Fat, 9% from Protein, 24% from Carb)		
Total Fat 16 g		
Saturated Fat 9 g		
Mono Fat 6 g		
Cholesterol 100 mg		
Sodium 156 mg		
Total Carbohydrate 13 g		
Dietary Fiber 0 g		
Sugars 0 g		
Protein 5 g		
Calcium 55 mg		
Iron 1 mg		

Cooked White Frosting

1 cup milk
5 tbsp. white flour
½ cup butter, softened
½ cup trans-fat-free shortening
1 cup sugar
1 tsp. vanilla extract

In saucepan, combine milk and flour. Cook on medium heat until mixture boils and thick paste forms, approximately 3-5 min. Cover and refrigerate until well chilled.

In mixing bowl with electric mixer, beat butter, shortening, sugar, and vanilla until creamy. Add chilled milk mixture. Beat at least 10 min. Spread over cake. Keep cake refrigerated.

Nutrition Facts	
Amount Per Total Recipe	
Calories 2,885 (60% from Fat, 4% from Protein, 36% from Carb)	
Total Fat 195 g	
Saturated Fat 84 g	
Mono Fat 70 g	
Cholesterol 256 mg	
Sodium 976 mg	
Total Carbohydrate 267 g	
Dietary Fiber 1 g	
Sugars 233 g	
Protein 26 g	
Calcium 790 mg	
Iron 3 mg	

Cream Cheese Frosting

3 oz. cream cheese, softened
1½ tbsp. cream or milk
¾ cups powdered sugar
1 tsp. vanilla extract

With electric mixer, beat cream cheese and cream or milk until soft and fluffy. Gradually beat in sugar. Add vanilla.

Note: This makes enough to frost the top of a Bundt cake.

Nutrition Facts	
Amount Per Total Recipe	
Calories 692 (43% from Fat, 4% from Protein, 53% from Carb)	
Total Fat 33 g	
Saturated Fat 21 g	
Mono Fat 9 g	
Cholesterol 106 mg	
Sodium 257 mg	
Total Carbohydrate 93 g	
Dietary Fiber 0 g	
Sugars 89 g	
Protein 7 g	
Calcium 77 mg	
Iron 1 mg	

Pudding Frosting

1 (1.5-oz.) pkg. sugar-free pudding (any
   flavor)
8 oz. frozen whipped topping, thawed
1½ cups cold milk

Whip together all ingredients with electric mixer. Will frost a 9x13-in. or 9-in. 2-layer cake.

Nutrition Facts		
Amount Per Total Recipe		
Calories 1,188 (44% from Fat, 12% from Protein, 44% from Carb)		
Total Fat 58 g		
Saturated Fat 50 g		
Mono Fat 4 g		
Cholesterol 18 mg		
Sodium 2305 mg		
Total Carbohydrate 132 g		
Dietary Fiber 1 g		
Sugars 99 g		
Protein 36 g		
Calcium 1207 mg		
Iron 1 mg		

Chocolate Glaze

3 tbsp. cocoa
2 tbsp. butter, melted
1 cup powdered sugar
2-3 tbsp. hot water

Combine all ingredients in bowl, and mix thoroughly with a spoon until smooth. Drizzle over cake.

Nutrition Facts		
Amount Per Total Recipe		
Calories 707 (30% from Fat, 2% from Protein, 68% from Carb)		
Total Fat 25 g		
Saturated Fat 16 g		
Mono Fat 7 g		
Cholesterol 61 mg		
Sodium 168 mg		
Total Carbohydrate 128 g		
Dietary Fiber 5 g		
Sugars 118 g		
Protein 3 g		
Calcium 29 mg		
Iron 2 mg		

Chocolate Chip Glaze

1 cup semi-sweet or sugar-free chocolate chips

Sprinkle chips on warm cupcakes as soon as they are removed from oven. Spread to frost. Yield: 12 servings.

Candy Bar Glaze

3 (1.5-oz.) sugar-free chocolate bars
Cream or cream cheese, optional
1 tbsp. butter, optional
Vanilla extract, optional

Melt chocolate. Add a bit of cream, cream cheese, and/or 1 tbsp. butter to this if you wish, to make it spread better. You can also add a bit of vanilla extract to enhance the flavor. Spread on top of cupcakes. Yield: 12 servings.

White Glaze

1 cup powdered sugar
1 tbsp. butter, softened
2 tbsp. milk

Combine all ingredients. Drizzle over cake.

Nutrition Facts	
Amount Per Total Recipe	
Calories 596 (17% from Fat, 2% from Protein, 81% from Carb)	
Total Fat 12 g	
Saturated Fat 7 g	
Mono Fat 3 g	
Cholesterol 32 mg	
Sodium 123 mg	
Total Carbohydrate 123 g	
Dietary Fiber 0 g	
Sugars 121 g	
Protein 3 g	
Calcium 99 mg	
Iron 0 mg	

Lemon Glaze

1 cup powdered sugar
4 tsp. fresh lemon juice

Whisk together. Drizzle over cake. Let cake sit approximately 20 min. until glaze is set.

Nutrition Facts	
Amount Per Total Recipe	
Calories 472 (0% from Fat, 0% from Protein, 100% from Carb)	
Total Fat 0 g	
Saturated Fat 0 g	
Mono Fat 0 g	
Cholesterol 0 mg	
Sodium 1 mg	
Total Carbohydrate 121 g	
Dietary Fiber 0 g	
Sugars 118 g	
Protein 0 g	
Calcium 3 mg	
Iron 0 mg	

Powdered Sugar Topping

Place a paper lace doily on top of cake. Sift powdered sugar over top. Carefully remove doily.

Chocolate Tuxedo Topping

2 squares (2 oz.) unsweetened chocolate
2 tsp. butter, softened

Melt together chocolate and butter in bowl set over hot water. Blend. Cool slightly.

Drizzle mixture from the tip of a spoon over top of a cake that has first been frosted all over with white frosting. Let some of the mixture run down sides. Keep cake in a cool place until chocolate is firm.

Nutrition Facts		
Amount Per Total Recipe		
Calories 352 (78% from Fat, 7% from Protein, 16% from Carb)		
Total Fat 37 g		
Saturated Fat 23 g		
Mono Fat 11 g		
Cholesterol 20 mg		
Sodium 68 mg		
Total Carbohydrate 17 g		
Dietary Fiber 9 g		
Sugars 1 g		
Protein 7 g		
Calcium 60 mg		
Iron 10 mg		

Chapter 9

Cookies and Bars

When we were newlyweds, my husband would occasionally ask if there was "something good" to eat in the house. This initially confused me, as our cupboards and fridge were always full of what I considered "something good" to eat. I soon realized he was referring to homemade desserts, and freshly baked cookies are among his favorites. My husband was also diagnosed with diabetes several years ago. These days, due to my improved culinary skills and diabetic-friendly baking, there is always "something good" to eat in the house.

A Norwegian proverb says, "Cookies are made of butter and love." I suppose this is why they make our mouths smile and our taste buds sing. Cookies are casual desserts, easy to make and bake, good any time of the day, already portioned, and portable. With these recipes, you can start filling the cookie jar again with all the old favorites: chocolate chip, peanut butter, oatmeal, and sugar cookies. They're all here and more enlightened, to fit into your new lifestyle.

To cut down on temptation, I recommend that you freeze your baked cookies in an airtight container and only remove a few as needed. They can be reheated in the microwave.

Soft Chocolate Chip Cookies

1 cup butter, softened, or 1 cup Smart Balance® regular spread

¾ cup brown sugar

1 (1.5-oz.) pkg. sugar-free instant vanilla pudding mix

2 eggs

1 tsp. vanilla extract

1 cup oat flour

1 cup white flour

¼ cup soy flour

1 tsp. baking soda

1 cup semi-sweet or sugar-free chocolate chips

1 cup pecan or walnut halves

In large bowl, cream together butter and sugar. Beat in pudding mix until blended. Add eggs and vanilla, and blend.

Sift together flours and baking soda. Add to wet ingredients, mixing until well incorporated. Stir in chips and nuts.

Drop by heaping teaspoonfuls on ungreased cookie sheets about 3 in. apart. Bake 10-12 min. at 350 degrees, or until edges are golden brown. Yield: 36 servings.

Nutrition Facts

Amount Per Serving

Calories 139 (61% from Fat, 5% from Protein, 34% from Carb)

Total Fat 9 g

  Saturated Fat 4 g

  Mono Fat 3 g

Cholesterol 27 mg

Sodium 128 mg

Total Carbohydrate 12 g

  Dietary Fiber 1 g

  Sugars 7 g

Protein 2 g

Calcium 17 mg

Iron 1 mg

Skillet Chocolate Chip Cookies

1 cup white whole-wheat flour

1 cup white flour

1 tsp. baking soda

½ tsp. salt

¾ cup butter, softened

¾ cup brown sugar

¼ cup Splenda®

1 egg

2 tsp. vanilla extract

1½ cups sugar-free or semi-sweet chocolate chips

½ cup chopped walnuts

Splenda® for dusting

No-sugar-added vanilla ice cream

Sugar-free chocolate syrup

Combine flours, baking soda, and salt. Set aside.

Cream together butter, brown sugar, and Splenda® until fluffy, approximately 2 min. Add egg and vanilla, and mix until combined.

Add flour mixture to butter mixture, and mix well. Add chips and nuts and combine.

Press ½ cup mixture into a seasoned, 5-in., ovenproof skillet (cast iron works well). Repeat with 7 more skillets. Bake approximately 20 min. in a preheated 350-degree oven, until cookies are brown but still a little soft in center.

Remove from oven and sprinkle top of each cookie with 1 tsp. Splenda®. Let cool a few minutes before carefully removing from pans. Top with ice cream and drizzle with syrup. Serve immediately. Yield: 16 servings.

Nutrition Facts		
Amount Per Serving		
Calories 278 (50% from Fat, 5% from Protein, 45% from Carb)		
Total Fat 16 g		
Saturated Fat 9 g		
Mono Fat 5 g		
Cholesterol 36 mg		
Sodium 221 mg		
Total Carbohydrate 33 g		
Dietary Fiber 2 g		
Sugars 19 g		
Protein 4 g		
Calcium 24 mg		
Iron 2 mg		

Whole-Wheat Oatie Chocolate Chip Cookies

¾ cup butter

¾ cup sugar

¾ cup brown sugar

1½ tsp. vanilla extract

2 eggs

2 cups whole-wheat or white whole-wheat flour

½ cup white flour

¾ tsp. baking soda

1 tsp. salt

1 cup rolled oats

1½ cups semi-sweet or sugar-free chocolate chips

½ cup chopped nuts, optional

Cream together butter and sugars with electric mixer. Mix in vanilla and eggs.

Sift flours, baking soda, and salt. Add oats and stir.

Gradually add flour mixture to butter mixture. Fold in chips and nuts if using.

Drop by teaspoonfuls onto greased cookie sheet about 3 in. apart. Bake approximately 8-10 min. at 375 degrees. Allow cookie sheet to cool 5 min. on wire rack. Remove cookies with spatula and cool completely on rack. Yield: 36 servings.

Nutrition Facts
Amount Per Serving
Calories 163 (41% from Fat, 7% from Protein, 53% from Carb)
Total Fat 8 g
Saturated Fat 4 g
Mono Fat 2 g
Cholesterol 24 mg
Sodium 127 mg
Total Carbohydrate 22 g
Dietary Fiber 2 g
Sugars 13 g
Protein 3 g
Calcium 15 mg
Iron 1 mg

Oatmeal Peanut Butter
Chocolate Chip Cookies

1 cup Smart Balance® regular spread

1 cup brown sugar

¾ cup Splenda®

1 cup peanut butter

2 eggs

1 cup white flour

¼ cup oat flour

2 tsp. baking soda

1 tsp. salt

1¼ cups rolled oats

1½ cups semi-sweet or sugar-free chocolate chips

Cream together spread, sugar, Splenda®, and peanut butter until smooth. Beat in eggs 1 at a time. In separate bowl, combine remaining ingredients. Stir into creamed mixture.

Drop by heaping teaspoonfuls onto ungreased cookie sheet about 3 in. apart. Bake approximately 17 min. in a preheated 325-degree oven. Let cookies firm up 3-4 min. on cookie sheet on wire rack. Remove with spatula and cool completely on wire rack. Yield: 60 servings.

Nutrition Facts

Amount Per Serving

Calories 77 (42% from Fat, 9% from Protein, 49% from Carb)

Total Fat 4 g

  Saturated Fat 1 g

  Mono Fat 2 g

Cholesterol 8 mg

Sodium 107 mg

Total Carbohydrate 10 g

  Dietary Fiber 1 g

  Sugars 6 g

Protein 2 g

Calcium 9 mg

Iron 1 mg

Oatmeal Cookies

1 cup Canola Butter (see index) or Smart Balance® regular spread

¾ cup packed brown sugar

1 (1.5-oz.) pkg. sugar-free instant vanilla pudding mix

2 eggs

1 tsp. vanilla extract

1¼ cups white flour or white whole-wheat flour

1 tsp. baking soda

1 tsp. cinnamon

½ tsp. salt

2½ cups rolled oats

1 cup raisins, optional

In large bowl, cream together butter and sugar until smooth. Blend in pudding mix. Add eggs and vanilla. Beat until light and fluffy.

Combine flour, baking soda, cinnamon, and salt. Add to batter. Stir in oats and raisins.

Drop by heaping teaspoonfuls onto cookie sheets lined with parchment paper, about 3 in. apart. Bake 8-12 min. in a preheated 350-degree oven, or until firm. Cool sheets on wire racks a few minutes. Remove cookies with spatula and cool completely on rack. Yield: 60 servings.

Nutrition Facts	
Amount Per Serving	
Calories 93 (26% from Fat, 7% from Protein, 66% from Carb)	
Total Fat 3 g	
Saturated Fat 1 g	
Mono Fat 1 g	
Cholesterol 14 mg	
Sodium 285 mg	
Total Carbohydrate 16 g	
Dietary Fiber 1 g	
Sugars 4 g	
Protein 2 g	
Calcium 18 mg	
Iron 1 mg	

Easy Peanut Butter Cookies

1 (18.25-oz.) pkg. yellow cake mix, regular or reduced sugar
1 cup peanut butter
½ cup canola oil
2 eggs
2 tbsp. water
Splenda® or sugar

Pour cake mix into large bowl and make a well in center. To the well, add peanut butter, oil, eggs, and water. Mix thoroughly.

Roll into small balls the size of marbles. Roll balls in Splenda® or sugar. Place about 2 in. apart on cookie sheet that has been sprayed with cooking spray. Bake 10-12 min. in a preheated 350-degree oven. Cool sheet several minutes on wire rack. Remove cookies with spatula and cool completely on rack. Yield: 36 servings.

Nutrition Facts		
Amount Per Serving		
Calories 110 (46% from Fat, 10% from Protein, 44% from Carb)		
Total Fat 6 g		
Saturated Fat 1 g		
Mono Fat 3 g		
Cholesterol 14 mg		
Sodium 135 mg		
Total Carbohydrate 13 g		
Dietary Fiber 1 g		
Sugars 7 g		
Protein 3 g		
Calcium 25 mg		
Iron 0 mg		

Sugar Cookies

¾ cup white flour

¾ cup white whole-wheat flour

1 tsp. baking powder

½ tsp. baking soda

⅔ tsp. nutmeg

1 stick butter, sliced

1 egg

½ cup sugar

1½ tbsp. milk

½ tsp. vanilla extract

Sugar for dipping

In large bowl, sift together flours, baking powder, baking soda, and nutmeg.

Cut in butter until crumbly.

Beat remaining ingredients until blended. Add to flour mixture.

Divide dough in half, cover, and chill in refrigerator several hours.

Roll dough out ¼ at a time on lightly floured board, to ⅛ in. thick. Cut with round 2½-in. cookie cutter and place on greased cookie sheets about 3-in. apart. Bake approximately 20 min. in a preheated 350-degree oven until pale golden.

Gently press tops of cookies into sugar while warm. Place cookies on wire racks to cool completely. Yield: 18 servings.

Nutrition Facts
Amount Per Serving
Calories 111 (45% from Fat, 6% from Protein, 49% from Carb)
Total Fat 6 g
Saturated Fat 3 g
Mono Fat 1 g
Cholesterol 27 mg
Sodium 105 mg
Total Carbohydrate 14 g
Dietary Fiber 1 g
Sugars 6 g
Protein 2 g
Calcium 25 mg
Iron 1 mg

Madeleines

8 tbsp. butter, softened
¾ cup powdered sugar, sifted
2 eggs
½ cup cake flour
½ cup white whole-wheat flour
¼ tsp. vanilla extract
Powdered sugar, sifted, for dusting

With electric mixer, beat butter until fluffy. Gradually beat in sugar. Add eggs 1 at a time, beating at high speed after each addition. Add flours and vanilla, and beat until blended.

Spoon 1 heaping tsp. into each well-buttered and floured madeleine cup. Bake approximately 20-25 min. in a preheated 350-degree oven until lightly browned. Release madeleines from cups by hitting the edge sharply against counter.

Cool. Sprinkle with sugar. Yield: 18 servings.

Note: Madeleines do not store well at room temperature and are best eaten the day they are made. They can be frozen.

Nutrition Facts

Amount Per Serving

Calories 99 (52% from Fat, 6% from Protein, 41% from Carb)

Total Fat 6 g

Saturated Fat 3 g

Mono Fat 2 g

Cholesterol 41 mg

Sodium 46 mg

Total Carbohydrate 10 g

Dietary Fiber 0 g

Sugars 5 g

Protein 2 g

Calcium 7 mg

Iron 1 mg

Sugarless Cookies

½ chopped cup dates

½ cup chopped peeled apples

1 cup raisins

1 cup water

3 eggs

½ cup trans-fat-free shortening or canola oil

½ cup pecans, walnuts, or almonds, chopped

1 tsp. baking soda

1 tsp. cinnamon

1 tsp. vanilla extract

½ tsp. salt

1⅓ cups whole-wheat or white whole-wheat flour

¼ cup Splenda® (optional)

In saucepan, combine dates, apples, raisins, and water. Simmer 3 min. Drain and cool.

Add remaining ingredients, and mix well by hand. Chill 15 min.

Drop by heaping teaspoonfuls on a greased cookie sheet, about 3 in. apart. Bake in a preheated 350-degree oven. Do not overbake.

Let sheet cool a few minutes on wire rack. Remove cookies with spatula and cool completely on rack. To prevent mold, store in cool place. Yield: 24 servings.

Nutrition Facts
Amount Per Serving
Calories 124 (47% from Fat, 7% from Protein, 46% from Carb)
Total Fat 7 g
Saturated Fat 1 g
Mono Fat 3 g
Cholesterol 31 mg
Sodium 113 mg
Total Carbohydrate 15 g
Dietary Fiber 2 g
Sugars 8 g
Protein 2 g
Calcium 16 mg
Iron 1 mg

Date Drops

½ cup Smart Balance® regular spread
¾ cup packed brown sugar
2 eggs
¼ cup milk
1 cup white flour
½ cup oat flour
1 tsp. baking powder
1 cup rolled oats
1 cup walnut halves, chopped
1 cup dates, chopped

Cream together spread and sugar. Add eggs and milk, and combine well. Sift together flours and baking powder. Add to wet ingredients gradually while mixing. Add oats, nuts, and dates.

Drop by teaspoonfuls onto an ungreased cookie sheet, about 2 in. apart. Bake 15-20 min. in a preheated 350-degree oven. Let sheet cool several minutes on wire rack. Remove drops with spatula and cool completely on rack. Yield: 30 servings.

Nutrition Facts

Amount Per Serving

Calories 136 (31% from Fat, 10% from Protein, 59% from Carb)

Total Fat 5 g	
Saturated Fat 1 g	
Mono Fat 2 g	
Cholesterol 16 mg	
Sodium 64 mg	
Total Carbohydrate 21 g	
Dietary Fiber 2 g	
Sugars 11 g	
Protein 4 g	
Calcium 35 mg	
Iron 1 mg	

Honey-Pecan Cookies

1 cup butter, softened
¼ cup honey or agave nectar
1 cup white flour, sifted
1 cup white whole-wheat flour, sifted
½ tsp. salt
2 tsp. vanilla extract
2 cups pecans, finely chopped
Powdered sugar

With electric mixer, cream butter. Gradually add honey or agave nectar, and mix well. Add flours, salt, and vanilla, and continue to mix well. Add nuts.

Roll into small balls, and place on a greased cookie sheet about 2 in. apart. Bake 40-45 min. in a preheated 400-degree oven. Remove from oven.

While warm, roll in sugar. Cool completely on wire racks. Yield: 96 servings.

Nutrition Facts		
Amount Per Serving		
Calories 46 (68% from Fat, 4% from Protein, 28% from Carb)		
Total Fat 4 g		
Saturated Fat 1 g		
Mono Fat 1 g		
Cholesterol 5 mg		
Sodium 26 mg		
Total Carbohydrate 3 g		
Dietary Fiber 0 g		
Sugars 1 g		
Protein 0 g		
Calcium 3 mg		
Iron 0 mg		

Russian Tea Cookies

1 cup butter, softened
½ cup powdered sugar, sifted
1 tsp. vanilla extract
1¼ cups all-purpose flour, sifted
1 cup white whole-wheat flour
¼ tsp. salt
¾ cup pecans, finely chopped
Powdered sugar for rolling

With electric mixer, combine butter, sugar, and vanilla. Sift flours together. Add flours and salt to butter mixture, and continue to mix. By hand, stir in nuts. Chill dough at least 1 hour.

Roll dough into 1-in. balls, and place on ungreased cookie sheets, about 1 in. apart. Bake approximately 17-20 min. in a preheated 350-degree oven until set, but not brown. While warm, roll in sugar. Let cool completely on wire racks. Roll in sugar again. Yield: 36 servings.

Nutrition Facts

Amount Per Serving

Calories 96 (63% from Fat, 4% from Protein, 33% from Carb)

Total Fat 7 g	
Saturated Fat 3 g	
Mono Fat 2 g	
Cholesterol 14 mg	
Sodium 53 mg	
Total Carbohydrate 8 g	
Dietary Fiber 1 g	
Sugars 2 g	
Protein 1 g	
Calcium 5 mg	
Iron 1 mg	

Holiday Nuggets

1 cup Canola Butter (see index) or Smart Balance® regular spread
½ cup powdered sugar, sifted
1 tbsp. vanilla extract
1 tsp. almond extract
1 cup white flour
1 cup white whole-wheat flour
½ tsp. salt
½ cup pecan halves, chopped
Powdered sugar for dusting
Colored crystallized sugar or Splenda® for dusting

In mixing bowl with electric mixer, cream together butter or spread and sugar. Blend in extracts. Gradually add to this the flours and salt. Stir in pecans.

Shape into 1¼-in. balls. Place on ungreased cookie sheets about 2 in. apart and flatten slightly with fingers. Bake 25 min. in a preheated 325-degree oven, or until bottoms are slightly browned.

Cool cookies on wire racks. Sprinkle with powdered sugar and then crystallized sugar or Splenda®. Yield: 42 servings.

Nutrition Facts

Amount Per Serving

Calories 63 (56% from Fat, 5% from Protein, 39% from Carb)

Total Fat 4 g
　Saturated Fat 2 g
　Mono Fat 1 g
Cholesterol 8 mg
Sodium 49 mg
Total Carbohydrate 6 g
　Dietary Fiber 1 g
　Sugars 2 g
Protein 1 g
Calcium 3 mg
Iron 0 mg

Shortbread

½ cup butter, softened
⅓ cup powdered sugar
¼ tsp. vanilla extract
½ cup white flour
½ cup white whole-wheat flour

With electric mixer at medium speed, cream butter until light. Add sugar and extract. Turn mixer to low speed and add flours, mixing just until combined.

Remove dough and press into bottom of a greased shortbread pan. Prick entire surface with a fork. Bake 30-35 min. in a preheated 325-degree oven, or until lightly browned, making sure center is thoroughly cooked. Let cool 10 min. before removing. Yield: 9 servings.

Note: A shortbread pan is a large, generally ceramic mold that imprints designs on shortbread cookies (usually holding 9 cookies). It is scored so that the cookies can be easily separated after baking.

Nutrition Facts	
Amount Per Serving	
Calories 158 (58% from Fat, 4% from Protein, 38% from Carb)	
Total Fat 10 g	
Saturated Fat 7 g	
Mono Fat 3 g	
Cholesterol 27 mg	
Sodium 73 mg	
Total Carbohydrate 15 g	
Dietary Fiber 1 g	
Sugars 4 g	
Protein 2 g	
Calcium 6 mg	
Iron 1 mg	

Applesauce Cookies

1 cup brown sugar
½ cup canola oil
1 egg, well beaten
1 cup unsweetened applesauce
1 tsp. baking soda
2 cups white whole-wheat flour
½ tsp. salt
½ tsp. nutmeg
½ tsp. cinnamon
¼ tsp. ground cloves
1 cup raisins
½ cup walnut halves, chopped

Cream together sugar and oil. Add egg and mix well. Add applesauce and baking soda, and continue to mix well. Add remaining ingredients and mix.

Drop by heaping spoonfuls onto greased cookie sheets, about 3 in. apart. Bake approximately 15-20 min. in a preheated 375-degree oven. Cool sheets several minutes on wire racks. Remove cookies with spatula and cool completely on racks. Yield: 36 servings.

Nutrition Facts
Amount Per Serving
Calories 76 (15% from Fat, 8% from Protein, 77% from Carb)
Total Fat 1 g
Saturated Fat 0 g
Mono Fat 0 g
Cholesterol 7 mg
Sodium 73 mg
Total Carbohydrate 15 g
Dietary Fiber 1 g
Sugars 9 g
Protein 2 g
Calcium 13 mg
Iron 1 mg

Buttermilk Cookies

COOKIES:

1 cup butter or trans-fat-free shortening, softened

1½ cups powdered sugar

2 eggs

½ cup buttermilk, well shaken

1¾ cups white flour

1¾ cups white whole-wheat flour

1 tsp. baking soda

1 tsp. salt

1 tsp. lemon zest

GLAZE:

1½ cups powdered sugar

3 tbsp. buttermilk, well shaken

½ tsp. vanilla extract

With electric mixer, cream together butter or shortening and sugar. Add eggs 1 at a time, and continue to beat. Add remaining ingredients and mix well.

Drop by rounded teaspoonfuls onto greased cookie sheets, about 3 in. apart. Bake 8-10 min. in a preheated 400-degree oven. Cool sheets several minutes on wire racks. Remove cookies with spatula and cool completely on racks.

Mix together all glaze ingredients. Brush on cooled cookies. Yield: 72 servings. Recipe can be halved.

Note: These cookies can be made with granulated sugar in lieu of powdered sugar.

Nutrition Facts
Amount Per Serving
Calories 68 (37% from Fat, 6% from Protein, 57% from Carb)
Total Fat 3 g
Saturated Fat 2 g
Mono Fat 1 g
Cholesterol 14 mg
Sodium 73 mg
Total Carbohydrate 10 g
Dietary Fiber 0 g
Sugars 5 g
Protein 1 g
Calcium 6 mg
Iron 0 mg

Chocolate Truffle Cookies

4 squares (1 oz. each) unsweetened chocolate

2 cups (12 oz.) semi-sweet or sugar-free chocolate chips, divided

⅓ cup butter or Smart Balance® regular spread

½ cup sugar

½ cup Splenda®

3 eggs

1½ tsp. vanilla extract

½ cup white or white whole-wheat flour

2 tbsp. unsweetened cocoa powder

¼ tsp. baking powder

¼ tsp. salt

Powdered sugar for dusting

In microwave or double boiler, melt chocolate, 1 cup chips, and butter. Mix. Cool 10 min.

In mixing bowl with electric mixer, beat sugar, Splenda®, and eggs 2 min. Beat in vanilla and the chocolate mixture. Combine flour, cocoa, baking powder, and salt. Gradually stir into chocolate mixture. By hand, stir in remaining chips. Cover and refrigerate at least 3 hours.

Roll into 1-in. balls with lightly floured hands. Place on an ungreased cookie sheet. Bake 10-12 min. in a preheated 350-degree oven, or until lightly puffed and set.

Cool sheet several minutes on wire rack until cookies are firm. Remove cookies with spatula and cool completely on rack. Dust with sugar. Yield: 48 servings.

Nutrition Facts	
Amount Per Serving	
Calories 77 (53% from Fat, 6% from Protein, 41% from Carb)	
Total Fat 5 g	
Saturated Fat 3 g	
Mono Fat 2 g	
Cholesterol 19 mg	
Sodium 30 mg	
Total Carbohydrate 9 g	
Dietary Fiber 1 g	
Sugars 6 g	
Protein 1 g	
Calcium 9 mg	
Iron 1 mg	

Double Chocolate Cookies

1¼ cups rolled oats
½ cup white flour
½ cup white whole-wheat flour
Pinch salt
½ tsp. baking powder
½ tsp. baking soda
7 oz. semi-sweet or sugar-free chocolate
½ cup butter, softened
½ cup sugar or Splenda®
½ cup brown sugar
1 egg, beaten
1 cup pecan halves, chopped

Spread oats on an ungreased cookie sheet and toast approximately 15 min. in a preheated 375-degree oven. Stir occasionally. Oats should be golden in color. Let cool.

Add oats to blender or food processor along with flours, salt, baking powder, and baking soda. Process until the texture of sand.

Finely grate 2 oz. chocolate, and with a sharp knife, chop remainder into large chunks.

With electric mixer, cream butter. Add sugars and/or Splenda® and continue beating until light and fluffy. Gradually add egg and continue beating 1 min.

Stir in oat mixture, chocolates, and pecans. Dough will be stiff.

Roll walnut-sized pieces of dough into balls by hand. Space about 3 in. apart on cookie sheets. Bake approximately 12 min. in a preheated 375-degree oven, or until firm.

Cool sheets several minutes on wire racks. Remove cookies with spatula and cool completely on racks. Yield: 30 servings.

Nutrition Facts		
Amount Per Serving		
Calories 154 (47% from Fat, 6% from Protein, 47% from Carb)		
Total Fat 8 g		
Saturated Fat 3 g		
Mono Fat 3 g		
Cholesterol 16 mg		
Sodium 66 mg		
Total Carbohydrate 19 g		
Dietary Fiber 2 g		
Sugars 11 g		
Protein 2 g		
Calcium 19 mg		
Iron 1 mg		

Finger Cookies

1 cup butter, softened
⅓ cup sugar
1¼ cups white flour
1¼ cups white whole-wheat flour
½ cup almonds, chopped
1 tsp. almond extract
Powdered sugar or Splenda®

In mixing bowl with electric mixer, cream together butter and sugar. Add flours, almonds, and almond extract. Take heaping tablespoonfuls of dough and roll into fingers. Chill dough at least 30 min.

Place on ungreased cookie sheets about 3 in. apart. Bake approximately 12-15 min. in a preheated 350-degree oven. While warm, roll in sugar or Splenda®. Cool on wire racks. Yield: 60 servings.

Nutrition Facts

Amount Per Serving

Calories 57 (57% from Fat, 6% from Protein, 37% from Carb)

Total Fat 4 g
 Saturated Fat 2 g
 Mono Fat 1 g
Cholesterol 8 mg
Sodium 22 mg
Total Carbohydrate 5 g
 Dietary Fiber 0 g
 Sugars 1 g
Protein 1 g
Calcium 5 mg
Iron 0 mg

Thumbprint Cookies

1 stick butter, softened
⅔ cup sugar
1 egg
1 tsp. vanilla extract
¾ cup white flour
¾ cup white whole-wheat flour
¼ tsp. baking soda
¼ tsp. salt
¼ cup walnut halves, finely chopped
⅓ cup sugar-free jam

In large bowl with electric mixer, cream butter until light and creamy. Add sugar and beat until smooth. Beat in egg and vanilla extract.

Sift together flours, baking soda, and salt. Add to butter mixture and blend. Stir in walnuts. Refrigerate dough 1 hour.

Roll dough into 1-in. balls. Place on a greased cookie sheet, approximately 2 in. apart. Make a deep indentation in center of each ball with thumb. Fill indentations with jam.

Bake approximately 15 min. in a preheated 350-degree oven, until edges are golden brown. Let sheet cool a few minutes on wire rack. Remove cookies with spatula and cool completely on rack. Yield: 18 servings.

Nutrition Facts

Amount Per Serving

Calories 133 (43% from Fat, 6% from Protein, 52% from Carb)

Total Fat 7 g	
Saturated Fat 3 g	
Mono Fat 2 g	
Cholesterol 27 mg	
Sodium 91 mg	
Total Carbohydrate 18 g	
Dietary Fiber 1 g	
Sugars 9 g	
Protein 2 g	
Calcium 7 mg	
Iron 1 mg	

Apricot Buttons

1 cup butter or Smart Balance® regular spread, softened
½ cup sugar or Splenda®
2 large eggs, separated
1 tsp. vanilla extract
1 cup white flour
1 cup white whole-wheat flour
½ tsp. salt
1½ cup finely ground walnuts
½ cup sugar-free apricot jam

In large bowl with electric mixer, beat butter and sugar or Splenda® until smooth. Add egg yolks and vanilla, and beat until well combined. Add flours and salt, and beat just until dough comes together.

In small bowl, beat egg whites until blended. Place walnuts in another small bowl. Shape dough into 1-in. balls. Dip each in egg whites, turning to coat completely. Roll in walnuts to coat.

Place balls about 1 in. apart on greased cookie sheets. Press thumb gently into center of each ball to make an imprint.

Bake 18-20 min. in a preheated 325-degree oven until lightly browned. Let sheets cool 5 min. and remove buttons to racks to cool completely. Fill each indentation with ½ tsp, jam. Yield: 36 servings.

Nutrition Facts

Amount Per Serving

Calories 208 (68% from Fat, 11% from Protein, 21% from Carb)

Total Fat 17 g	
Saturated Fat 4 g	
Mono Fat 4 g	
Cholesterol 27 mg	
Sodium 74 mg	
Total Carbohydrate 12 g	
Dietary Fiber 2 g	
Sugars 4 g	
Protein 6 g	
Calcium 17 mg	
Iron 1 mg	

Strawberry Pockets

8 oz. cream cheese, softened
1 cup Smart Balance® regular spread or Canola Butter (see index)
1 cup white flour
1 cup white whole-wheat flour
½ cup no-sugar-added strawberry or other fruit preserves
Powdered sugar

With electric mixer, combine cream cheese and spread or butter until well blended. Add flours and continue to mix.

Roll out dough on a lightly floured board to ⅛-in. thickness. Cut with 2½-in. round cookie cutter. Place on ungreased cookie sheets about 2 in. apart. Add ¼ tsp. preserves in center of each circle. Moisten edges with a bit of cold water. Fold in half and seal edges.

Bake 14-16 min. in a preheated 375-degree oven, or until lightly browned. Remove from oven and sprinkle each with sugar. Remove pockets with spatula and cool completely on wire racks. Yield: 42 servings.

Nutrition Facts	
Amount Per Serving	
Calories 63 (56% from Fat, 7% from Protein, 37% from Carb)	
Total Fat 4 g	
Saturated Fat 2 g	
Mono Fat 1 g	
Cholesterol 6 mg	
Sodium 69 mg	
Total Carbohydrate 6 g	
Dietary Fiber 0 g	
Sugars 1 g	
Protein 1 g	
Calcium 7 mg	
Iron 0 mg	

Fig Bars

½ cup trans-fat-free shortening

1 cup sugar

1 egg

½ cup milk

1 tsp. vanilla extract

½ tsp. salt

1½ cups white flour

1½ cups whole-wheat or white whole-wheat flour

1 tbsp. baking powder

1 cup figs, chopped

½ cup Splenda®

½ cup hot water

With electric mixer, cream together shortening and sugar. Add egg and beat until light.

In small bowl, combine milk and vanilla extract; set aside.

Sift together salt, flours, and baking powder. Add alternately with milk to creamed mixture. Blend well.

Roll out into a 12x14-in. rectangle approximately ⅛ in. thick on a slightly floured board.

Place figs and Splenda® in a small saucepan with water and boil 5 min. Cool.

Spread fig mixture over half the dough to within 1 in. of edges. Cover with remaining half of dough, press edges together lightly to seal, and cut with knife or pastry wheel into 4 strips, 3½ in. wide x 12 in. long. Cut each strip into 10 pieces.

Place on ungreased cookie sheet about 1 in. apart. Bake 12-15 min. in a preheated 400-degree oven. Cool sheet completely on wire rack. Yield: 40 servings.

Nutrition Facts
Amount Per Serving
Calories 89 (28% from Fat, 6% from Protein, 66% from Carb)
Total Fat 3 g
Saturated Fat 1 g
Mono Fat 1 g
Cholesterol 6 mg
Sodium 72 mg
Total Carbohydrate 15 g
Dietary Fiber 0 g
Sugars 6 g
Protein 1 g
Calcium 33 mg
Iron 1 mg

Bonbon Cookies

½ cup butter, softened
¾ cup powdered sugar, sifted
1 tbsp. vanilla extract
¾ cup white flour
¾ cup white whole-wheat flour
⅛ tsp. salt
1-2 tbsp. milk or cream, optional
Nuts for filling

FROSTING:
1 cup sifted powdered sugar
2 tbsp. cream or half and half
1 tsp. vanilla extract
Food coloring, optional

With electric mixer, thoroughly combine butter, sugar, and vanilla.

By hand, mix in flours and salt. If dough appears dry, add milk or cream.

Wrap 1 level tbsp. dough around various nuts such as whole almonds, walnuts, and pecans.

Place 1 in. apart on an ungreased cookie sheet. Bake approximately 12-15 min. in a preheated 350-degree oven until set but not brown.

Combine frosting ingredients. Dip tops of warm cookies into frosting. Cool completely on wire rack. Yield: 24 servings.

Nutrition Facts	
Amount Per Serving	
Calories 101 (37% from Fat, 4% from Protein, 59% from Carb)	
Total Fat 4 g	
Saturated Fat 3 g	
Mono Fat 1 g	
Cholesterol 11 mg	
Sodium 42 mg	
Total Carbohydrate 15 g	
Dietary Fiber 1 g	
Sugars 9 g	
Protein 1 g	
Calcium 8 mg	
Iron 0 mg	

Potato Chip Cookies

1 cup butter or Smart Balance® regular spread, softened
½ cup sugar
1 tsp. vanilla extract
½ cup crushed potato chips
½ cup pecan halves, chopped
1 cup white flour
1 cup white whole-wheat flour

Cream together butter or spread, sugar, and vanilla. Add potato chips and pecans. Stir in flours.

Form into small balls. Place on ungreased cookie sheets about 2 in. apart and press cookies flat. Bake 15 min. in a preheated 350-degree oven.

Cool sheets several minutes on wire racks. Remove cookies with spatula and cool completely on racks. Yield: 36 servings.

Nutrition Facts

Amount Per Serving

Calories 109 (60% from Fat, 4% from Protein, 36% from Carb)

Total Fat 7 g	
Saturated Fat 4 g	
Mono Fat 2 g	
Cholesterol 14 mg	
Sodium 55 mg	
Total Carbohydrate 10 g	
Dietary Fiber 1 g	
Sugars 3 g	
Protein 1 g	
Calcium 5 mg	
Iron 0 mg	

Marbled American Brownies

1 (12.35-oz.) pkg. reduced-sugar brownie mix
½ cup walnut halves, chopped
3 oz. regular or light cream cheese, softened
2½ tbsp. butter, softened
⅙ cup (2 tbsp. + 2 tsp.) sugar
1 egg
1 tbsp. flour
⅓ tsp. vanilla extract
½ (16-oz.) tub reduced-sugar chocolate frosting
Chopped walnuts

Prepare brownie mix according to pkg. directions, adding ½ cup chopped walnuts. Spread half of batter in a greased 8x8-in. pan.

Beat together cream cheese and butter. Add sugar, egg, flour, and vanilla and beat until smooth. Pour over brownie batter in pan.

Drop remaining brownie batter in spots over cream cheese mixture in pan. Swirl mixtures together with a knife.

Bake 30-35 min. in a preheated 350-degree oven. Cool and frost. Sprinkle with nuts. Cut into small squares. Yield: 18 servings.

Nutrition Facts

Amount Per Serving

Calories 245 (55% from Fat, 3% from Protein, 42% from Carb)

Total Fat 15 g	
Saturated Fat 7 g	
Mono Fat 4 g	
Cholesterol 34 mg	
Sodium 142 mg	
Total Carbohydrate 26 g	
Dietary Fiber 0 g	
Sugars 19 g	
Protein 2 g	
Calcium 11 mg	
Iron 1 mg	

Quick Brownie

4 tbsp. packaged brownie mix

2 tbsp. milk, plain yogurt, or sour cream

1 tbsp. chopped walnuts or pecans, optional

Grease an individual ramekin and add all ingredients. Stir until well combined.

Microwave 30-60 seconds. Yield: 1 serving.

Nutrition Facts		
Amount Per Serving		
Calories 133 (30% from Fat, 14% from Protein, 56% from Carb)		
Total Fat 5 g		
Saturated Fat 0 g		
Mono Fat 1 g		
Cholesterol 2 mg		
Sodium 43 mg		
Total Carbohydrate 20 g		
Dietary Fiber 2 g		
Sugars 11 g		
Protein 5 g		
Calcium 100 mg		
Iron 1 mg		

Congo Squares

⅔ cup butter or Canola Butter (see index)

1⅛ cups dark brown sugar

1⅛ cups Splenda®

1 cup white flour

1 cup white whole-wheat flour

¾ cup oat flour

2½ tsp. baking powder

½ tsp. salt

3 eggs, beaten

1 tbsp. vanilla extract

2 cups semi-sweet or sugar-free chocolate chips

1 cup walnut or pecan halves, chopped

In saucepan, melt butter over medium heat. Stir in sugar and Splenda®. Cool slightly.

Add flours, baking powder, and salt. Add eggs. Stir in vanilla, chips, and nuts. Batter will be very stiff.

Spread into a greased and floured 12x9x2-in. baking pan. Bake 25-30 min. in a preheated 350-degree oven. Cut into squares while warm. Yield: 48 squares.

Note: You may use 2¼ cups Splenda® Brown Sugar Blend instead of brown sugar and Splenda®.

Nutrition Facts	
Amount Per Serving	
Calories 131 (45% from Fat, 6% from Protein, 49% from Carb)	
Total Fat 7 g	
Saturated Fat 3 g	
Mono Fat 2 g	
Cholesterol 22 mg	
Sodium 76 mg	
Total Carbohydrate 17 g	
Dietary Fiber 1 g	
Sugars 9 g	
Protein 2 g	
Calcium 29 mg	
Iron 1 mg	

Whoopie Pies

1 (18.25-oz.) pkg. chocolate cake mix, regular or reduced sugar
1 stick butter, softened
½ cup powdered sugar or Splenda®
2 cups sugar-free marshmallow creme
1½ tsp. vanilla extract

Prepare mix according to pkg. directions, except use only ¾ cup water.

Using a cookie or ice cream scoop, drop batter onto greased or parchment-lined cookie sheets in 2½- to 3-in. circles.

Bake approximately 12 min. in a preheated 350-degree oven, or until toothpick inserted in centers comes out clean. Cool.

In medium bowl with electric mixer set to medium speed, beat together butter, sugar or Splenda®, and marshmallow creme. Stir in vanilla.

Spread half the chocolate cakes with this filling. Top with remaining cakes to form sandwiches. Yield: 24 servings.

Note: Sugar-free marshmallow creme can be purchased through www.amazon.com.

Nutrition Facts

Amount Per Serving

Calories 184 (44% from Fat, 6% from Protein, 50% from Carb)

Total Fat 8 g	
Saturated Fat 3 g	
Mono Fat 3 g	
Cholesterol 41 mg	
Sodium 217 mg	
Total Carbohydrate 22 g	
Dietary Fiber 1 g	
Sugars 12 g	
Protein 2 g	
Calcium 37 mg	
Iron 1 mg	

Chapter 10

Pies and Tarts

Pies typically consist of a filling and a crust. They can be fried, baked, refrigerated, or frozen. Dessert pies contain some sort of sweet filling, of course. Pie fillings generally consist of nuts, fruits, creams, or custards.

Traditional piecrusts are made of flour, fat, and water but can be fashioned from other ingredients as well. The purpose of the crust is to house and protect the filling, while adding a complementary taste and texture to the finished dessert. Good cooks pride themselves on their ability to produce a tender, golden, flaky piecrust, as piecrusts can be tricky to master. It is possible to do so, though, given time, patience, and sufficient practice.

My mom was most known in the baking department for making exceptional pies from scratch. She would bake all manner of pies. But I most remember my sister and me as kids making our yearly forays into the late-summer woods to gather big, dark, juicy berries from the blackberry brambles. These would be presented to my mother, who would use them to bake her luscious blackberry cobblers— both tangy and sweet, with the hot, syrupy juice flowing over the crust. We were big dessert eaters in our house, with homemade desserts being the satisfying finale to most evening meals. I continue this tradition to this day, though my desserts are now much lower in carbs.

As with other desserts, pies can be portion controlled by preparing individual tarts. I find that artificial sweeteners work exceedingly well in most pies. You might prefer to prepare a one-crust or lattice-crust pie, to minimize the carbs or white flour if using in your piecrusts.

Double Piecrust

2 cups white flour
1 tsp. Splenda® or sugar
1 tsp. salt
1 tsp. baking powder
1 stick butter, sliced
½ cup trans-fat-free shortening
½ cup cold water

Mix together dry ingredients. Cut in butter and shortening with 2 knives or a pastry blender until crumbs are pea sized. Add cold water and stir until dough forms. Separate into 2 disks. Roll each out on a lightly floured board or between 2 sheets of plastic or waxed paper. Bake as directed in pie recipes calling for a double crust. Yield: 1 9- or 10-in. double piecrust.

Note: You may substitute ½ cup white whole-wheat flour or oat flour for ½ cup white flour. Half all-purpose and half whole-wheat pastry flour can also be used. Butter-flavor Crisco® works well in this recipe.

Nutrition Facts

Amount Per Total Recipe

Calories 2,716 (65% from Fat, 3% from Protein, 32% from Carb)

Total Fat 197 g	
Saturated Fat 84 g	
Mono Fat 70 g	
Cholesterol 244 mg	
Sodium 3507 mg	
Total Carbohydrate 216 g	
Dietary Fiber 5 g	
Sugars 1 g	
Protein 23 g	
Calcium 340 mg	
Iron 21 mg	

White Whole-Wheat Double Piecrust

2 cups white whole-wheat flour
1 tsp. salt
¾ cup trans-fat-free shortening
4-8 tsp. ice water

Mix together flour and salt. Cut in shortening with 2 crisscrossed knives or a pastry blender until crumbs are pea sized. Sprinkle in water and mix with a fork until dough holds together.

Separate into 2 disks and flatten each. Roll each out on a lightly floured board or between 2 sheets of plastic or waxed paper to fit pie pan. Bakeas directed in pie recipes calling for a double crust. Yield: 1 9- or 10-in. double piecrust.

Note: Whole-wheat pastry flour can be substituted for a flakier crust. Half all-purpose flour and half whole-wheat pastry flour can also be used.

Nutrition Facts		
Amount Per Total Recipe		
Calories 2,173 (63% from Fat, 6% from Protein, 31% from Carb)		
Total Fat 158 g		
Saturated Fat 39 g		
Mono Fat 69 g		
Cholesterol 0 mg		
Sodium 2370 mg		
Total Carbohydrate 174 g		
Dietary Fiber 29 g		
Sugars 1 g		
Protein 33 g		
Calcium 83 mg		
Iron 9 mg		

Graham Cracker Piecrust

2 tbsp. butter
2 tbsp. warm water
3 tbsp. Splenda®
1 cup graham cracker crumbs

In medium saucepan, melt butter. Remove from heat and add water and Splenda®. Stir in graham cracker crumbs.

Press firmly into bottom and sides of an 8- or 9-in. pie plate. Bake 6-8 min. at 400 degrees or until nicely browned. Yield: 1 piecrust.

Nutrition Facts

Amount Per Total Recipe

Calories 1,051 (37% from Fat, 5% from Protein, 58% from Carb)

Total Fat 43 g	
Saturated Fat 18 g	
Mono Fat 13 g	
Cholesterol 61 mg	
Sodium 1471 mg	
Total Carbohydrate 153 g	
Dietary Fiber 7 g	
Sugars 46 g	
Protein 14 g	
Calcium 164 mg	
Iron 8 mg	

Baked Nut Piecrust

1½ cups ground pecans or walnuts
3 tbsp. butter, softened
2 tbsp. Splenda®

Combine all ingredients in medium mixing bowl. Press firmly into bottom and sides of a 9-in. pie plate. Bake approximately 10 min. in a preheated 325-degree oven or until edges are golden brown. Cool before filling. Yield: 1 piecrust.

Nutrition Facts		
Amount Per Total Recipe		
Calories 1,452 (89% from Fat, 4% from Protein, 7% from Carb)		
Total Fat 153 g		
Saturated Fat 32 g		
Mono Fat 76 g		
Cholesterol 92 mg		
Sodium 245 mg		
Total Carbohydrate 26 g		
Dietary Fiber 16 g		
Sugars 7 g		
Protein 15 g		
Calcium 125 mg		
Iron 4 mg		

Cheddar Cheese Piecrust

1 cup white flour
1 cup white whole-wheat flour
1 tsp. salt
⅔ cup trans-fat free shortening
¾ cup shredded sharp cheddar cheese
5 tbsp. water or more

In medium bowl, mix together flours, salt, and shortening with 2 criss-crossed knives or a pastry blender, until mixture resembles coarse cornmeal. Stir in cheese.

Add water gradually, and mix with fork. Shape into 2 disks. Roll out on lightly floured board to fit 9-in. pie plate. Yield: 1 double piecrust. For use with apple pie.

Nutrition Facts		
Amount Per Total Recipe		
Calories 2,510 (61% from Fat, 8% from Protein, 31% from Carb)		
Total Fat 173 g		
Saturated Fat 56 g		
Mono Fat 70 g		
Cholesterol 104 mg		
Sodium 2981 mg		
Total Carbohydrate 195 g		
Dietary Fiber 17 g		
Sugars 1 g		
Protein 52 g		
Calcium 775 mg		
Iron 15 mg		

Bumbleberry Pie

½ cup sugar

½ cup Splenda®

5 tbsp. white or whole-wheat flour

2 tbsp. cornstarch

½ tsp. cinnamon

¼ tsp. nutmeg

1 cup blackberries

1 cup blueberries

1 cup sliced strawberries

1 cup raspberries

1 9-in. double piecrust

1 tbsp. butter, sliced into small pieces

1 tsp. sugar, optional

Combine sugar, Splenda®, flour, cornstarch, cinnamon, and nutmeg and mix well.

Add fruit and lightly mix. Pour into piecrust.

Dot with butter. Cover with top crust. Prick top crust with a fork. Sprinkle evenly with 1 tsp. sugar, if desired.

Bake 50 min. at 375 degrees or until golden brown. Yield: 8 servings.

Nutrition Facts		
Amount Per Serving		
Calories 353 (42% from Fat, 5% from Protein, 53% from Carb)		
Total Fat 17 g		
Saturated Fat 5 g		
Mono Fat 7 g		
Cholesterol 4 mg		
Sodium 245 mg		
Total Carbohydrate 48 g		
Dietary Fiber 5 g		
Sugars 17 g		
Protein 4 g		
Calcium 22 mg		
Iron 2 mg		

Brown Bag Apple Pie

PIE:

8-10 McIntosh apples, peeled and quartered

1 tbsp. lemon juice

½ cup Splenda® or sugar

2 tbsp. flour

½ tsp. cinnamon

1 9-in. unbaked piecrust

TOPPING:

½ cup sugar

½ cup flour

1 stick butter, sliced

In large bowl, toss together apples, lemon juice, Splenda® or sugar, flour, and cinnamon. Pour into piecrust.

For topping, combine sugar and flour. Sprinkle topping over pie. Dot with butter.

Place pie in large brown bag and fold several times to seal. Place on baking sheet. Bake 1 hour in a preheated 425-degree oven. Yield: 12 servings.

Nutrition Facts
Amount Per Serving
Calories 250 (46% from Fat, 3% from Protein, 51% from Carb)
Total Fat 13 g
Saturated Fat 6 g
Mono Fat 4 g
Cholesterol 20 mg
Sodium 136 mg
Total Carbohydrate 33 g
Dietary Fiber 2g
Sugars 17 g
Protein 2 g
Calcium 10 mg
Iron 1 mg

Down Under Apple Pie

PIE:

6 tart cooking apples

1 cup Splenda®

2 tbsp. whole-wheat or whole-wheat pastry flour

1 tsp. cinnamon

1 tsp. lemon zest

⅛ tsp. ground cloves

⅛ tsp. salt

1 9-in. unbaked piecrust in deep-dish pie plate, edges fluted

TOPPING:

½ cup whole-wheat or whole-wheat pastry flour

¼ cup sugar

⅛ tsp. salt

½ cup grated cheddar cheese

¼ cup melted butter

Light sour cream

Peel, quarter, and core apples before slicing thin. Combine Splenda®, flour, cinnamon, lemon zest, cloves, and salt. Toss apples lightly in this mixture. Arrange apples in piecrust, overlapping slices.

For topping, combine flour, sugar, salt, and cheese. Mix in butter. Sprinkle this mixture over apples.

Bake 40 min. at 400 degrees, or until both crust and topping are golden brown. Serve warm with dollop of sour cream. Yield: 8 servings.

Nutrition Facts	
Amount Per Serving	
Calories 320 (46% from Fat, 6% from Protein, 48% from Carb)	
Total Fat 17 g	
Saturated Fat 8 g	
Mono Fat 6 g	
Cholesterol 25 mg	
Sodium 289 mg	
Total Carbohydrate 40 g	
Dietary Fiber 3 g	
Sugars 16 g	
Protein 5 g	
Calcium 78 mg	
Iron 1 mg	

Sour Cream Apple Pie

4 large apples, peeled and sliced
½ cup sugar or Splenda®
½ tsp. cinnamon
3 tbsp. flour
16 oz. sour cream
1 9-in. unbaked piecrust

Mix apples with sugar or Splenda®, cinnamon, flour, and sour cream. Pour into piecrust. Bake 1 hour in a preheated 375-degree oven. Serve warm. Refrigerate any leftovers. Yield: 8 servings.

Nutrition Facts		
Amount Per Serving		
Calories 286 (45% from Fat, 5% from Protein, 50% from Carb)		
Total Fat 15 g		
Saturated Fat 6 g		
Mono Fat 5 g		
Cholesterol 22 mg		
Sodium 145 mg		
Total Carbohydrate 36 g		
Dietary Fiber 1 g		
Sugars 19 g		
Protein 4 g		
Calcium 67 mg		
Iron 1 mg		

Crustless Apple Pie

2 tsp. cinnamon

3 tbsp. brown sugar

6 apples, sliced

1 cup water

⅓ cup whole-wheat flour

½ cup white flour

1 tsp. baking powder

½ tsp. salt

6 tbsp. butter

Mix together cinnamon and brown sugar. Add half this mixture, with apples and water, to a saucepan. Cook over medium heat until almost tender, approximately 10 min.

In a bowl, stir together flours, baking powder, and salt. Melt butter. Cut into dry ingredients with remaining cinnamon-sugar mixture until crumbly.

Turn apple mixture into a 9-in. pie plate. Sprinkle crumbs on top. Bake 35-40 min. at 350 degrees. Yield: 8 servings.

Nutrition Facts		
Amount Per Serving		
Calories 192 (40% from Fat, 4% from Protein, 56% from Carb)		
Total Fat 9 g		
Saturated Fat 6 g		
Mono Fat 2 g		
Cholesterol 23 mg		
Sodium 272 mg		
Total Carbohydrate 28 g		
Dietary Fiber 2 g		
Sugars 15 g		
Protein 2 g		
Calcium 55 mg		
Iron 1 mg		

Pineapple Pie

1 (20-oz.) can crushed pineapple in syrup
¾ cup Splenda®
½ tsp. cinnamon
¼ tsp. nutmeg
2 tbsp. cornstarch
1 double piecrust
Butter
Milk
Sparkling sugar, optional

In medium saucepan, stir together pineapple, Splenda®, cinnamon, nutmeg, and cornstarch. Heat to boiling and cook 2-3 min. Remove from heat when thickened. Let cool a bit.

Pour into unbaked piecrust. Dot with butter and add top piecrust. Seal.

Brush top of crust with small amount of milk. Sprinkle with a bit of sparkling sugar, if desired. Bake 1 hour at 375 degrees, or until crust is brown. Yield: 8 servings.

Note: Sparkling sugar, such as the Wilton® brand, can be purchased in specialty food stores that carry cake-decorating supplies. It is sprinkled on top of pies and cookies to make them sparkle.

This pie can also be made with 2 cans crushed pineapple. You'll need to double the Splenda®, cinnamon, nutmeg, and cornstarch.

Nutrition Facts

Amount Per Serving

Calories 267 (46% from Fat, 4% from Protein, 50% from Carb)

Total Fat	14 g
Saturated Fat	4 g
Mono Fat	7 g
Cholesterol	4 mg
Sodium	303 mg
Total Carbohydrate	34 g
Dietary Fiber	1 g
Sugars	9 g
Protein	3 g
Calcium	36 mg
Iron	1 mg

Peach Schnapps Pie

2 (1 lb. 13-oz.) cans sliced peaches, drained
1 tsp. cinnamon
¾ tsp. nutmeg
½ cup brown sugar
¾ cup peach schnapps
3 tbsp. flour
1 tbsp. cornstarch
1 tbsp. lemon juice
1 double piecrust
Butter
Milk
1 tsp. sugar

In bowl, gently combine first 8 ingredients, ending with lemon juice.

Fit bottom piecrust into 8x8-in. square baking dish or 9-in. pie plate. Pour in peach mixture. Dot with butter.

Add top crust and seal. Vent top of pie by pricking with fork in several places. Brush crust with a little milk, and sprinkle top with 1 tsp. sugar.

Bake 40 min. at 400 degrees, or until top is golden brown. Serve warm with no-sugar-added ice cream.
Yield: 16 servings.

Nutrition Facts	
Amount Per Serving	
Calories 217 (37% from Fat, 4% from Protein, 59% from Carb)	
Total Fat 9 g	
Saturated Fat 2 g	
Mono Fat 4 g	
Cholesterol 2 mg	
Sodium 134 mg	
Total Carbohydrate 31 g	
Dietary Fiber 3 g	
Sugars 17 g	
Protein 2 g	
Calcium 13 mg	
Iron 1 mg	

Nantucket Cranberry Crisp

FILLING:

6 cups frozen cranberries

½ cup walnut halves, chopped

½ cup Splenda®

TOPPING:

2 eggs, beaten

½ cup flour

½ cup sugar

Combine filling ingredients. Pour into a greased shallow ceramic pan.

Combine topping ingredients. Add topping to pan. Bake 30-40 min. in a preheated 350-degree oven, until glossy and crisp. Yield: 12 servings.

Nutrition Facts	
Amount Per Serving	
Calories 129 (29% from Fat, 8% from Protein, 64% from Carb)	
Total Fat 4 g	
Saturated Fat 1 g	
Mono Fat 1 g	
Cholesterol 41 mg	
Sodium 15 mg	
Total Carbohydrate 21 g	
Dietary Fiber 3 g	
Sugars 11 g	
Protein 3 g	
Calcium 15 mg	
Iron 1 mg	

Fabulous Fruit Pies

1 (20-oz.) can light pie filling (blueberry, blackberry, apple, cherry, etc.)
¼ cup Splenda®
½ tsp. cinnamon
¼ tsp. nutmeg
1 9-in. double piecrust
Butter
Milk, optional
Sparkling sugar, optional

In bowl, gently but thoroughly combine pie filling, Splenda®, cinnamon, and nutmeg.

Line pie plate with piecrust and prick bottom. Add filling and dot with butter. Add top crust and seal. Prick top with fork. Brush with a little milk and sprinkle a little sparkling sugar on top, if desired.

Bake approximately 1 hour in a preheated 375-degree oven, or until crust is golden brown. Yield: 8 servings.

Nutrition Facts

Amount Per Serving

Calories 249 (49% from Fat, 5% from Protein, 45% from Carb)

Total Fat 14 g	
Saturated Fat 4 g	
Mono Fat 7 g	
Cholesterol 4 mg	
Sodium 310 mg	
Total Carbohydrate 28 g	
Dietary Fiber 2 g	
Sugars 7 g	
Protein 3 g	
Calcium 34 mg	
Iron 1 mg	

Blueberry Cobbler

2 cups blueberries

⅓ cup Splenda®

⅛ tsp. cinnamon

½ cup cake flour

½ cup white whole-wheat flour

1 tsp. baking powder

1 tsp. salt

1 egg

⅔ cup sugar

¼ cup trans-fat-free shortening

½ cup milk

½ tsp. cinnamon

Combine berries with Splenda® and cinnamon. Spread evenly in a greased 8x8-in. baking dish.

Sift together flours, baking powder, and salt, and set aside. In food processor or blender, combine remaining ingredients 1 min. Pour over sifted flour mixture. Stir just until mixed. Spread this batter over berries.

Bake approximately 35 min. in a preheated 375-degree oven, or until done. Serve warm with milk, cream, or no-sugar-added ice cream. Yield: 9 servings.

Note: Other fruits such as cherries, peaches, plums, or strawberries can be substituted for blueberries.

Nutrition Facts
Amount Per Serving
Calories 202 (29% from Fat, 7% from Protein, 64% from Carb)
Total Fat 7 g
Saturated Fat 2 g
Mono Fat 3 g
Cholesterol 28 mg
Sodium 344 mg
Total Carbohydrate 33 g
Dietary Fiber 2 g
Sugars 20 g
Protein 4 g
Calcium 83 mg
Iron 1 mg

Strawberry Cobbler

6 cups whole strawberries, hulled
⅓ cup Splenda®
2 cups whole-wheat pastry flour
⅔ cup sugar
2 tsp. baking powder
¼ tsp. baking soda
¼ tsp. salt
¾ cup butter
1 cup buttermilk
Powdered sugar, sifted

Lightly grease a 9x13-in. baking dish. Place strawberries in dish and sprinkle with Splenda®; set aside.

In large bowl, sift together flour, sugar, baking powder, baking soda, and salt. Cut in butter until mixture is coarse and crumbly. Add buttermilk and stir until blended. With wooden spoon, beat approximately 30 seconds until a very thick batter forms.

Drop batter in dollops over strawberries. Spread batter over strawberries with back of spoon as best you can. Do not worry about any holes in batter.

Bake approximately 35 min. in a preheated 375-degree oven, until golden brown. Remove from oven and sprinkle with sugar. Serve warm. Yield: 12-16 servings.

Nutrition Facts

Amount Per Serving

Calories 273 (39% from Fat, 6% from Protein, 55% from Carb)

Total Fat 12 g	
Saturated Fat 8 g	
Mono Fat 3 g	
Cholesterol 31 mg	
Sodium 248 mg	
Total Carbohydrate 40 g	
Dietary Fiber 5 g	
Sugars 15 g	
Protein 4 g	
Calcium 85 mg	
Iron 2 mg	

Blueberry Tartlets

3 tbsp. sugar
1⅓ cups white flour
1 cup white whole-wheat flour
¾ tsp. salt
⅔ cup cold butter, sliced
2 tbsp. fresh lemon juice
3 tbsp. ice water
1 pt. blueberries, washed
2 tbsp. honey
1 tbsp. lemon zest
Whipped cream for garnish

In bowl, combine sugar, flours, and salt. Cut in butter with 2 crisscrossed knives or a pastry blender until mixture is texture of coarse cornmeal. Add lemon juice and water. Gather dough into a ball. Flatten slightly between 2 sheets of waxed paper. Refrigerate 1 hour.

Roll out dough on a lightly floured board to about ¼-in. thickness. Cut into 5-in. circles. Place circles into 12 large ungreased muffin cups. Prick bottoms and sides with a fork.

Bake 15 min. in a preheated 400-degree oven, or until golden. If air bubbles appear while baking, prick with the point of a knife as they appear. Cool slightly. Remove tart shells from pan.

Combine berries, honey, and lemon zest. Fill each shell. Top each with dollop of whipped cream. Yield: 12 servings.

Nutrition Facts

Amount Per Serving

Calories 217 (43% from Fat, 5% from Protein, 52% from Carb)

Total Fat 11 g	
Saturated Fat 7 g	
Mono Fat 3 g	
Cholesterol 27 mg	
Sodium 221 mg	
Total Carbohydrate 29 g	
Dietary Fiber 2 g	
Sugars 9 g	
Protein 3 g	
Calcium 11 mg	
Iron 2 mg	

Mexican Fruit Pies

6 small whole-wheat tortillas
1 (20-oz.) can light apple, cherry, or peach pie filling
3 tbsp. canola oil
Powdered sugar for dusting

Soften tortillas in microwave approximately 10 seconds. Place 2 tbsp. pie filling in center of each tortilla. Fold over sides, and then close ends.

Heat oil in skillet. Place pies seam side down in skillet. Cook over medium-high heat until golden, turning once.

Drain on paper towels. Dust with sugar. Yield: 6 servings.

Nutrition Facts

Amount Per Serving

Calories 184 (60% from Fat, 3% from Protein, 37% from Carb)

Total Fat 9 g	
Saturated Fat 0 g	
Mono Fat 4 g	
Cholesterol 0 mg	
Sodium 11 mg	
Total Carbohydrate 22 g	
Dietary Fiber 9 g	
Sugars 9 g	
Protein 4 g	
Calcium 10 mg	
Iron 0 mg	

Grapefruit Pie

¾ cup Splenda®
3 tbsp. cornstarch
½ cup water or grapefruit juice
1 (3–oz.) box sugar-free strawberry or lemon Jell-O®
2 ruby-red grapefruits, peeled and sectioned, or 1 can
1 9-in. piecrust, baked and cooled
Whipped cream for garnish

In medium saucepan, combine Splenda® with cornstarch. Add water or grapefruit juice. Cook over medium heat approximately 6-7 min. until thick and clear.

Add Jell-O®, and stir until dissolved. Let cool.

Add grapefruit.

Pour mixture into piecrust. Chill until firm, approximately 2 hours. Serve with whipped cream. Yield: 8 servings.

Nutrition Facts		
Amount Per Serving		
Calories 200 (37% from Fat, 16% from Protein, 47% from Carb)		
Total Fat 8 g		
Saturated Fat 2 g		
Mono Fat 3 g		
Cholesterol 0 mg		
Sodium 365 mg		
Total Carbohydrate 23 g		
Dietary Fiber 1 g		
Sugars 4		
Protein 8 g		
Calcium 18 mg		
Iron 1 mg		

Strawberry Yogurt Pie

16 oz. plain yogurt
1½ cups crushed strawberries
¾-1 cup Splenda®
8- or 9 oz. frozen whipped topping, thawed
1 graham cracker piecrust
Whole strawberries for garnish
Mint leaves for garnish

Mix together first 4 ingredients. Spread in graham cracker crust and freeze, covered, 4 hours. Remove from freezer ½ hour before serving. Garnish with strawberries and mint. Yield: 8 servings.

Nutrition Facts		
Amount Per Serving		
Calories 300 (49% from Fat, 5% from Protein, 46% from Carb)		
Total Fat 17 g		
Saturated Fat 9 g		
Mono Fat 4 g		
Cholesterol 7 mg		
Sodium 204 mg		
Total Carbohydrate 35 g		
Dietary Fiber 1 g		
Sugars 23 g		
Protein 4 g		
Calcium 84 mg		
Iron 1 mg		

Pumpkin Pie

3 eggs, beaten
1¾ cups pumpkin puree
¾ cup sugar or Splenda®
½ tsp. salt
1 tsp. cinnamon
¼ tsp. ginger
¼ tsp. nutmeg
1½ pt. no-sugar-added vanilla ice cream, softened
2 unbaked piecrusts
Whipped cream for garnish

Beat eggs lightly. Stir in pumpkin puree, sugar, salt, and spices. Add ice cream and blend until ice cream is fully melted and batter is smooth. Pour into piecrusts.

Bake 15 min. in a preheated 425-degree oven. Lower heat to 350 degrees. Bake an additional 30-40 min. or until set.

Serve with dollop of whipped cream. Yield: 16 servings.

Nutrition Facts		
Amount Per Serving		
Calories 200 (39% from Fat, 8% from Protein, 53% from Carb)		
Total Fat 9 g		
Saturated Fat 3 g		
Mono Fat 4 g		
Cholesterol 50 mg		
Sodium 258 mg		
Total Carbohydrate 27 g		
Dietary Fiber 2 g		
Sugars 13 g		
Protein 4 g		
Calcium 74 mg		
Iron 1 mg		

Sweet Potato Pie

4 large hot sweet potatoes, peeled, chopped and mashed
4 tbsp. butter, melted
1 cup Splenda®
1 cup sugar
1 tsp. nutmeg
½ tsp. cinnamon
4 eggs
⅓ cup evaporated milk
1 tsp. vanilla extract
2 9-in. unbaked piecrusts
Whipped cream for garnish

In large mixing bowl with electric mixer, combine all filling ingredients until smooth. Pour into piecrusts.

Bake 10 min. in a preheated 450-degree oven. Lower heat to 350 degrees. Bake an additional 30 min. or until set.

Serve with dollop of whipped cream. Yield: 16 servings.

Nutrition Facts		
Amount Per Serving		
Calories 236 (40% from Fat, 7% from Protein, 53% from Carb)		
Total Fat 11 g		
Saturated Fat 4 g		
Mono Fat 5 g		
Cholesterol 69 mg		
Sodium 203 mg		
Total Carbohydrate 32 g		
Dietary Fiber 1 g		
Sugars 16 g		
Protein 4 g		
Calcium 47 mg		
Iron 1 mg		

German Chocolate Pie

1 (4-oz.) pkg. German sweet chocolate
¼ cup butter
1⅔ cups evaporated milk
1 cup Splenda®
½ cup sugar
3 tbsp. cornstarch
⅛ tsp. salt
2 eggs
1 tsp. vanilla extract
1 10-in. or 2 8-in. unbaked piecrust(s)
⅓ cup flaked coconut
½ cup pecan halves

In medium saucepan over low heat, melt chocolate and butter. Stir until blended. Remove from heat. Gradually stir in milk.

Mix together Splenda®, sugar, cornstarch, and salt. Beat in eggs and vanilla extract. Gradually blend in chocolate mixture. Pour into piecrust(s).

Combine coconut and nuts, and sprinkle over filling. Bake 45 min. in a preheated 375-degree oven. The filling will be soft but will set as it cools. It is important to let set 4 hours before cutting. Store leftovers in refrigerator. Yield: 16 servings.

Nutrition Facts

Amount Per Serving

Calories 219 (52% from Fat, 8% from Protein, 41% from Carb)

Total Fat 13 g
　Saturated Fat 5 g
　Mono Fat 5 g
Cholesterol 39 mg
Sodium 141 mg
Total Carbohydrate 23 g
　Dietary Fiber 1 g
　Sugars 13 g
Protein 4 g
Calcium 85 mg
Iron 1 mg

Chocolate Chiffon Pie

¼ cup cocoa powder

½ cup sugar or Splenda®

3 eggs, separated

1 env. plain gelatin

¼ cup water

1 cup whipping cream, whipped

1 9-in. graham cracker piecrust

In top of double boiler over medium heat, mix together cocoa, sugar or Splenda®, and egg yolks. Cook until thick. Soften gelatin in ¼ cup water. Add to cocoa mixture. Cool.

Beat egg whites until stiff. Fold into mixture. Fold in whipped cream. Pour mixture into piecrust and chill 3 hours until firm. Yield: 8 servings.

Nutrition Facts

Amount Per Serving

Calories 281 (45% from Fat, 8% from Protein, 47% from Carb)

Total Fat 15 g	
Saturated Fat 5 g	
Mono Fat 6 g	
Cholesterol 109 mg	
Sodium 209 mg	
Total Carbohydrate 34 g	
Dietary Fiber 1 g	
Sugars 24 g	
Protein 6 g	
Calcium 32 mg	
Iron 1 mg	

Chocolate Pie in Meringue Shell

SHELL:

2 egg whites

½ tsp. vinegar

½ tsp. water

⅛ tsp. salt

½ cup sugar or Splenda®

½ tsp. vanilla extract

FILLING:

¾ cup semi-sweet or sugar-free chocolate chips

3 tbsp. hot water

1 cup whipping cream, whipped stiff

For shell, beat egg whites until stiff. Add vinegar, water, and salt. Beat lightly.

Add sugar or Splenda® very gradually. Add vanilla. Beat until stiff but not dry.

Spread mixture into bottom and sides of a well-greased 9-in. pie plate. Bake 1 hour in a preheated 250-degree oven. Cool.

For filling, melt chocolate chips and water in double boiler over hot water. Cool. Fold into whipped cream.

Spread filling evenly in cooled meringue shell. Additional whipped cream may be spread on top if desired. Chill in refrigerator at least 1 hour. Yield: 8 servings.

Nutrition Facts
Amount Per Serving
Calories 173 (46% from Fat, 4% from Protein, 50% from Carb)
Total Fat 9 g
Saturated Fat 6 g
Mono Fat 3 g
Cholesterol 17 mg
Sodium 58 mg
Total Carbohydrate 23 g
Dietary Fiber 1 g
Sugars 21 g
Protein 2 g
Calcium 16 mg
Iron 1 mg

Black Forest Pie

8 oz. frozen whipped topping, thawed
1 chocolate wafer piecrust
1 cup cold milk
1 (1.5-oz.) pkg. sugar-free instant chocolate pudding mix
1 cup light cherry pie filling

Spread 1 cup whipped topping on bottom of piecrust.

In medium bowl, combine milk and pudding mix. Blend with wire whisk 1 min. Fold in 1½ cups whipped topping. Spread this mixture over whipped topping in piecrust.

Spread remaining whipped topping over top, leaving a 1-in. border around edge and creating a depression in center of whipped topping. Spoon cherry pie filling into center depression. Chill at least 2 hours. Yield: 8 servings.

Nutrition Facts

Amount Per Serving

Calories 291 (49% from Fat, 7% from Protein, 45% from Carb)

Total Fat 16 g	
Saturated Fat 8 g	
Mono Fat 5 g	
Cholesterol 2 mg	
Sodium 392 mg	
Total Carbohydrate 33 g	
Dietary Fiber 1 g	
Sugars 20 g	
Protein 5 g	
Calcium 115 mg	
Iron 1 mg	

Coconut Cream Pie

3 cups half and half

2 eggs

¾ cup Splenda®

½ cup white whole-wheat flour

¼ tsp. salt

1 cup flaked coconut, toasted in oven

1 tsp. vanilla extract

1 9-in. piecrust, baked

1 cup Sweetened Whipped Cream (see index) or frozen whipped topping, thawed

In medium saucepan, combine half and half, eggs, Splenda®, flour, and salt. Over medium heat, bring to a boil, stirring constantly. Remove from heat. Add ¾ cup coconut and the vanilla.

Pour into piecrust. Chill approximately 2-4 hours until firm.

Top with whipped cream or topping and remaining coconut. Yield: 8 servings.

Nutrition Facts		
Amount Per Serving		
Calories 375 (64% from Fat, 8% from Protein, 28% from Carb)		
Total Fat 27 g		
Saturated Fat 14 g		
Mono Fat 8 g		
Cholesterol 112 mg		
Sodium 256 mg		
Total Carbohydrate 26 g		
Dietary Fiber 2 g		
Sugars 0 g		
Protein 8 g		
Calcium 120 mg		
Iron 1 mg		

Peanut Butter Pie

2¾ pt. no-sugar-added vanilla ice cream, softened slightly
½ cup peanut butter
2 oz. semi-sweet or sugar-free chocolate chips
1 graham cracker piecrust
Chocolate Sauce (see index)
Sweetened Whipped Cream (see index)
Chopped peanuts for garnish

By hand, stir together ice cream, peanut butter, and chocolate chips. Spoon into crust. Freeze immediately until solid, approximately 2 hours, or overnight. Drizzle chocolate sauce over pie, add dollop of whipped cream, and sprinkle with nuts. Yield: 16 servings.

Note: I use Healthy Choice® low-fat, no-sugar-added ice cream to make this recipe.

Nutrition Facts		
Amount Per Serving		
Calories 207 (50% from Fat, 9% from Protein, 41% from Carb)		
Total Fat 12 g		
Saturated Fat 4 g		
Mono Fat 5 g		
Cholesterol 8 mg		
Sodium 166 mg		
Total Carbohydrate 22 g		
Dietary Fiber 2 g		
Sugars 12 g		
Protein 5 g		
Calcium 96 mg		
Iron 1 mg		

Lemonade Ice Cream Pie

⅓ cup sugar-free lemonade mix (such as Country Time®)
½ cup water
1 pt. no-sugar-added vanilla ice cream, softened
2 tbsp. lemon zest
1 (8-oz.) container frozen whipped topping, thawed
1 9-in. graham cracker piecrust

In large bowl, dissolve lemonade mix in water. Add ice cream and stir until smooth. Add zest and whipped topping and stir until combined.

Spread into piecrust and freeze at least 4 hours. Yield: 10 servings.

Nutrition Facts		
Amount Per Serving		
Calories 230 (51% from Fat, 4% from Protein, 44% from Carb)		
Total Fat 13 g		
Saturated Fat 7 g		
Mono Fat 3 g		
Cholesterol 4 mg		
Sodium 166 mg		
Total Carbohydrate 26 g		
Dietary Fiber 1 g		
Sugars 17 g		
Protein 2 g		
Calcium 59 mg		
Iron 1 mg		

Cheesecake Pie

1 (8-oz.) pkg. cream cheese, softened
8 oz. sour cream
¾ cup milk
1 (1.5-oz.) pkg. sugar-free instant vanilla pudding mix
1 9-in. graham cracker piecrust

Cream together cream cheese and sour cream. Add milk and pudding mix, and continue to cream until smooth. Pour into piecrust. Chill until firm, approximately 3 hours. Top with your favorite topping, if desired. Yield: 8 servings.

Nutrition Facts

Amount Per Serving

Calories 323 (57% from Fat, 8% from Protein, 35% from Carb)

Total Fat 21 g	
Saturated Fat 10 g	
Mono Fat 7 g	
Cholesterol 43 mg	
Sodium 517 mg	
Total Carbohydrate 29 g	
Dietary Fiber 1 g	
Sugars 15 g	
Protein 6 g	
Calcium 137 mg	
Iron 1 mg	

Chapter 11

Puddings and Such

I'm surprised whenever I encounter someone who tells me they don't like custards. Upon further questioning, they generally reveal it's the texture they don't particularly care for. I don't get it, I truly don't. I mean, what's not to like? Its viscosity? That smooth velvety sensation running over the tongue and around the mouth feels downright sensual to me. Not to mention, it also tastes pretty darn good. I absolutely love custards. I feel there's no finer dessert than a well-made caramelized crème brûlée and no more comforting ending to a meal than an old-fashioned baked rice pudding dotted with raisins. Did you know that rice pudding was traditionally prescribed for the young and infirm, and the formula was inscribed in medical texts before it appeared in cookbooks? I imagine there must have been a lot of folks pretending to be sick in those days!

I cut carbs in many of my custard recipes by mixing whole milk with water and by using half sugar and half Splenda®. A sprinkle of cinnamon also nicely enhances custards.

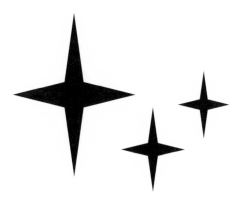

Vanilla Custard

3 tbsp. cornstarch
⅔ cup Splenda®
1¼ cups evaporated milk
1¼ cups water
2 eggs, beaten
1½ tsp. vanilla extract

In medium saucepan, combine cornstarch, Splenda®, evaporated milk, water, and eggs. Whisk until smooth. Cook over medium heat, stirring, until custard is thick and bubbly. Cook 1 more min. Remove from heat.

Stir in vanilla. Pour into bowl or serving dishes. Cover with plastic wrap, and chill 2-3 hours. Serve with whipped cream, if desired. Yield: 6 servings.

Note: To use as pie filling, add 1 more tbsp. cornstarch when cooking.

Nutrition Facts
Amount Per Serving
Calories 128 (43% from Fat, 19% from Protein, 38% from Carb)
Total Fat 6 g
Saturated Fat 3 g
Mono Fat 2 g
Cholesterol 97 mg
Sodium 83 mg
Total Carbohydrate 12 g
Dietary Fiber 0 g
Sugars 0 g
Protein 6 g
Calcium 147 mg
Iron 0 mg

Double Chocolate Custard

3 tbsp. cornstarch
¾ cup Splenda®
2 tbsp. cocoa powder
1¼ cups evaporated milk
1¼ cups water
1 egg, beaten
⅓ cup sugar-free or semi-sweet chocolate chips
1½ tsp. vanilla extract
Whipped cream

In medium saucepan, combine cornstarch, Splenda®, cocoa, milk, water, and egg. Whisk until smooth. Cook over medium heat, stirring until custard is thick and bubbly. Cook 1 more min. Remove from heat and stir in chocolate chips; whisk until melted. Stir in vanilla.

Cover with plastic wrap and chill 2-3 hours. Serve with whipped cream. Yield: 6 servings.

Nutrition Facts		
Amount Per Serving		
Calories 164 (42% from Fat, 13% from Protein, 45% from Carb)		
Total Fat 8 g		
Saturated Fat 5 g		
Mono Fat 3 g		
Cholesterol 56 mg		
Sodium 71 mg		
Total Carbohydrate 19 g		
Dietary Fiber 1 g		
Sugars 5 g		
Protein 6 g		
Calcium 148 mg		
Iron 1 mg		

Coconut Custard

2 eggs
½ cup Splenda®
2 tsp. coconut extract
Dash nutmeg
2 cups milk, scalded
Whipped cream
Toasted coconut for garnish

In large bowl, lightly beat eggs. Add Splenda®, coconut extract, and nutmeg. Blend in hot milk.

Pour into small, greased, 1-qt. casserole dish. Bake 1 hour in a preheated 325-degree oven. Serve with whipped cream topped with a little toasted coconut. Yield: 4 servings.

Nutrition Facts		
Amount Per Serving		
Calories 102 (53% from Fat, 22% from Protein, 24% from Carb)		
Total Fat 6 g		
Saturated Fat 3 g		
Mono Fat 2 g		
Cholesterol 133 mg		
Sodium 66 mg		
Total Carbohydrate 6 g		
Dietary Fiber 0 g		
Sugars 3 g		
Protein 6 g		
Calcium 87 mg		
Iron 1 mg		

Pumpkin Custard

1 cup pumpkin puree
¼ cup sugar
½ cup Splenda®
⅛ tsp. allspice
¼ tsp. nutmeg
¼ tsp. salt
3 eggs, lightly beaten
1½ cups milk, scalded
Whipped cream

Combine pumpkin, sugar, Splenda®, allspice, nutmeg, salt, and eggs. Add milk slowly while stirring constantly. Pour into 6 greased custard cups.

Set in pan of warm water. Bake approximately 40 min. in a preheated 350-degree oven, or until knife inserted in centers comes out clean. Serve with whipped cream. Yield: 6 servings.

Nutrition Facts

Amount Per Serving

Calories 116 (31% from Fat, 17% from Protein, 52% from Carb)

Total Fat 4 g
  Saturated Fat 2 g
  Mono Fat 1 g
Cholesterol 126 mg
Sodium 153 mg
Total Carbohydrate 15 g
  Dietary Fiber 1 g
  Sugars 12 g
Protein 5 g
Calcium 61 mg
Iron 1 mg

Crème Brûlée

3 cups whipping cream
6 egg yolks
⅓ cup Splenda®
1 tsp. vanilla extract
⅓ cup brown sugar, packed

Heat cream in 1-qt. saucepan over medium heat until small bubbles form around edge of pan.

Meanwhile, in larger saucepan and using a wire whisk, blend egg yolks with Splenda®. Slowly stir in cream.

Over medium-low heat, cook mixture, stirring constantly, until it just coats the back of a metal spoon. Do not boil. This will take approximately 15 min. Remove from heat. Stir in vanilla.

Pour mixture into an ungreased, 1½-qt., broiler-safe casserole dish. Refrigerate at least 6 hours.

Preheat broiler. Sift brown sugar over chilled custard. Broil 3-4 min. until sugar melts. Refrigerate. May be served with sliced fruit of your choice. Yield: 10 servings.

Nutrition Facts
Amount Per Serving
Calories 188 (75% from Fat, 5% from Protein, 20% from Carb)
Total Fat 16 g
Saturated Fat 9 g
Mono Fat 5 g
Cholesterol 172 mg
Sodium 21 mg
Total Carbohydrate 9 g
Dietary Fiber 0 g
Sugars 7 g
Protein 2 g
Calcium 42 mg
Iron 0 mg

Flan

1¾ cups Splenda®
½ cup water
3 eggs
5 egg yolks
2 (12-oz.) cans regular or fat-free evaporated milk
2 tsp. vanilla extract
2 cups fresh fruit
1 tbsp. Grand Marnier®, optional

Fill large bowl with ice water. Set aside.

In a 2-qt. flan pan, over medium-high heat, combine 1 cup Splenda® with ½ cup water. Boil but do not stir this mixture—simply swirl the pan around. Cook until the caramel turns a deep amber color, approximately 3 min.

Remove pan from heat. Set in the bowl of ice water to arrest cooking, moving the pan around so the caramel coats the sides. Leave pan in water until mixture is hard and starts to crack. Set aside.

In large mixing bowl, combine eggs, egg yolks, remaining Splenda®, evaporated milk, and vanilla. Whisk until well combined. Pour this mixture through a strainer and into flan pan. Cover tightly with foil.

Place flan pan into another pan that has been filled halfway with hot water.

Bake 1¼ hours in a preheated 350-degree oven, or until firm. Remove from oven and let cool 20 min.

Refrigerate overnight.

Remove flan from refrigerator. Unmold on large serving platter with at least a 2-in. border. Arrange fruit around and on top of flan.

In small pan, heat Grand Marnier® until warm. Drizzle over flan and serve at once. Yield: 16 servings.

Nutrition Facts

Amount Per Serving

Calories 84 (28% from Fat, 27% from Protein, 45% from Carb)

Total Fat 3 g	
Saturated Fat 1 g	
Mono Fat 1 g	
Cholesterol 112 mg	
Sodium 67 mg	
Total Carbohydrate 9 g	
Dietary Fiber 0 g	
Sugars 6 g	
Protein 6 g	
Calcium 139 mg	
Iron 1 mg	

Strawberry Panna Cotta

1 lb. strawberries
1¾ cups buttermilk, well shaken
6 tbsp. sugar or Splenda®
1 env. plain gelatin
¼ cup whole milk, half and half, or sour cream
¼ cup whipping cream
Strawberries for garnish

In blender, blend strawberries, buttermilk, and sugar or Splenda® until smooth. Pour through a small sieve into a bowl, pressing hard on solids. Discard solids.

In small bowl, sprinkle gelatin over milk, half and half, or sour cream. Let sit 1 min. to soften.

In small saucepan, bring cream to a boil. Remove from heat and add gelatin mixture; stir until dissolved. Whisk cream mixture into strawberry mixture. Pour into mold or molds.

Chill panna cotta until firm, at least 8 hours. To unmold, set mold or molds 2-3 min. in a bowl that contains a little hot water.

Before serving, let stand at room temperature 20 min. to soften. Garnish with berries. Yield: 6 servings.

Nutrition Facts

Amount Per Serving

Calories 117 (22% from Fat, 11% from Protein, 68% from Carb)

Total Fat 3 g	
Saturated Fat 2 g	
Mono Fat 1 g	
Cholesterol 10 mg	
Sodium 38 mg	
Total Carbohydrate 21 g	
Dietary Fiber 2 g	
Sugars 18 g	
Protein 3 g	
Calcium 73 mg	
Iron 0 mg	

Baked Rice Pudding

3 eggs, lightly beaten
3 cups milk
1 tsp. vanilla extract
½ cup sugar
½ cup Splenda®
3 tbsp. melted butter
½ cup raisins or dried cranberries
1 cup cooked brown rice
½ tsp. cinnamon
Nutmeg

Blend together all ingredients except nutmeg, mixing well. Pour into an ungreased, 1½-qt. casserole dish. Sprinkle top with nutmeg.

Place casserole dish in larger pan. Add hot water to about halfway up pudding pan.

Bake 35-40 min. in a preheated 400-degree oven, or until knife inserted in center comes out clean. Can be served warm or cold. Refrigerate any leftovers. Yield: 8 servings.

Note: Be very careful handling the pan of hot water. It is best to use long cooking mitts when handling.

Nutrition Facts		
Amount Per Serving		
Calories 212 (34% from Fat, 10% from Protein, 56% from Carb)		
Total Fat 8 g		
Saturated Fat 4 g		
Mono Fat 2 g		
Cholesterol 108 mg		
Sodium 81 mg		
Total Carbohydrate 30 g		
Dietary Fiber 1 g		
Sugars 21 g		
Protein 5 g		
Calcium 74 mg		
Iron 1 mg		

Apple Brown Betty

2 cups whole-wheat or oatmeal breadcrumbs
¼ cup butter, melted
8 apples, peeled, cored, and sliced (about 6 cups)
½ cup sugar or Splenda®
½ tsp. nutmeg
¼ tsp. cinnamon
1½ tbsp. lemon juice
1 tbsp. lemon zest
½ cup water

Combine breadcrumbs and butter. Spread ⅓ in bottom of a greased 1½-qt. casserole dish. Cover with half the apples.

Combine sugar or Splenda®, spices, juice, zest, and water. Cover apple layer with half this mixture. Top with half the remaining breadcrumbs, all the remaining apples, and all the remaining sugar or Splenda® mixture. Top with remaining breadcrumbs.

Cover with foil. Bake 30 min. in a preheated 375-degree oven. Remove cover and bake 30 min. more, or until apples are tender. Serve warm with cream, if desired. Yield: 16 servings.

Note: Peeled and sliced peaches may be substituted for the apples. This recipe also can be made with Splenda® Brown Sugar Blend.

Nutrition Facts

Amount Per Serving

Calories 116 (26% from Fat, 5% from Protein, 69% from Carb)

Total Fat 4 g	
Saturated Fat 2 g	
Mono Fat 1 g	
Cholesterol 8 mg	
Sodium 94 mg	
Total Carbohydrate 21 g	
Dietary Fiber 2 g	
Sugars 16 g	
Protein 2 g	
Calcium 15 mg	
Iron 1 mg	

Coffee Bread Pudding

½ cup oatmeal bread cubes
1½ cups hot milk
1½ cups strong brewed black coffee
2 eggs, beaten
⅓ cup sugar
⅓ cup Splenda®
¼ tsp. salt
1 tbsp. butter
1 tsp. vanilla extract
½ cup chopped nuts

Combine all ingredients. Pour into buttered 1½-qt. casserole dish. Bake 35-40 min. in a preheated 350-degree oven, or until firm. Yield: 8 servings.

Nutrition Facts

Amount Per Serving

Calories 150 (50% from Fat, 12% from Protein, 38% from Carb)

Total Fat 9 g	
Saturated Fat 2 g	
Mono Fat 2 g	
Cholesterol 67 mg	
Sodium 134 mg	
Total Carbohydrate 15 g	
Dietary Fiber 2 g	
Sugars 10 g	
Protein 5 g	
Calcium 80 mg	
Iron 1 mg	

Stovetop Chocolate Bread Pudding

1 square unsweetened chocolate

1½ cups milk

2 cups crust-trimmed oatmeal bread cubes

¼ cup sugar or Splenda®

⅛ tsp. salt

1 tsp. vanilla extract

8 large marshmallows, quartered

In double boiler over simmering water, melt chocolate in milk. Add bread cubes, sugar or Splenda®, and salt. Stir gently until thickened; it will only take a moment.

Remove from heat. Stir in vanilla and marshmallows. Serve warm with cream, if desired. Yield: 4 servings.

Nutrition Facts

Amount Per Serving

Calories 140 (23% from Fat, 12% from Protein, 65% from Carb)	
Total Fat 4 g	
Saturated Fat 2 g	
Mono Fat 1 g	
Cholesterol 2 mg	
Sodium 203 mg	
Total Carbohydrate 24 g	
Dietary Fiber 3 g	
Sugars 11 g	
Protein 4 g	
Calcium 59 mg	
Iron 2 mg	

Eclair Squares

ECLAIR BASE:

1 cup water

½ cup butter

½ cup white flour

½ cup white whole-wheat flour

4 eggs, beaten

TOPPING:

2 (1.5-oz.) pkg. sugar-free instant vanilla pudding mix

4 cups cold milk

8 oz. cream cheese, softened

8 oz. frozen whipped topping, thawed

Chocolate syrup

For base, in saucepan, bring water and butter to a boil, stirring until butter is melted. Turn off heat, but leave saucepan on burner. Add flours, stirring until smooth and blended. Add eggs and mix well. Spread mixture in a greased 17x11-in. jellyroll pan.

Bake approximately 30 min. in a preheated 400-degree oven, or until golden brown. Cool and smooth out any air bubbles.

For topping, prepare pudding using only 3 cups milk. In blender, blend together remaining milk and cream cheese. Add to pudding mixture.

Spread on top of cooled base. Let sit 10 min. in refrigerator. Top with whipped topping and drizzle with chocolate syrup. Yield: 24 servings.

Nutrition Facts

Amount Per Serving

Calories 154 (65% from Fat, 9% from Protein, 26% from Carb)

Total Fat 11 g	
Saturated Fat 7 g	
Mono Fat 3 g	
Cholesterol 63 mg	
Sodium 227 mg	
Total Carbohydrate 10 g	
Dietary Fiber 0 g	
Sugars 3 g	
Protein 3 g	
Calcium 44 mg	
Iron 1 mg	

Layered Pudding Squares

15 whole graham crackers
1 (2.1-oz.) pkg. sugar-free instant vanilla pudding mix
2 cups cold milk
1 cup frozen whipped topping, thawed
1 (20-oz.) can light cherry pie filling

Line a 9x9-in. square pan with ⅓ of the graham crackers, breaking some if necessary. Prepare pudding mix with milk as directed on pudding pkg. Let stand 5 min.

Blend in whipped topping. Spread half the pudding mixture on top of crackers. Add a second cracker layer with half of the remaining crackers. Top with remaining pudding mixture. Top with remaining crackers.

Spread cherry pie filling over top layer of crackers. Chill 3 hours. Yield: 9 servings.

Nutrition Facts
Amount Per Serving
Calories 194 (26% from Fat, 7% from Protein, 68% from Carb)
Total Fat 6 g
Saturated Fat 3 g
Mono Fat 1 g
Cholesterol 3 mg
Sodium 438 mg
Total Carbohydrate 33 g
Dietary Fiber 2 g
Sugars 17 g
Protein 3 g
Calcium 53 mg
Iron 1 mg

Oreo® Cheesecake Dessert

1 (18-oz.) pkg. Oreo® cookies or 3 (6.75-oz.) pkg. sugar-free
    Oreo® cookies
½ cup butter
16 oz. frozen whipped topping, thawed
8 oz. light cream cheese, softened
1 cup powdered sugar
1 (2.1-oz.) pkg. sugar-free instant chocolate pudding mix
2 cups milk

Crush Oreos® into bite-size pieces, reserving 1 cup for top. Melt butter and mix with rest of cookies. Press into 9x13-in. baking pan or slightly smaller. Put in freezer for 5 min.

Blend half the whipped topping with all the cream cheese and sugar. Spread over crust. Place cheesecake back in freezer.

Prepare pudding with milk according to pkg. directions. Spread over top of cheesecake. Spread remaining whipped topping on top of pudding. Sprinkle with remaining crushed cookies. Keep cheesecake refrigerated. Yield: 16 servings.

Nutrition Facts	
Amount Per Serving	
Calories 280 (58% from Fat, 4% from Protein, 38% from Carb)	
Total Fat 18 g	
Saturated Fat 12 g	
Mono Fat 4 g	
Cholesterol 25 mg	
Sodium 276 mg	
Total Carbohydrate 27 g	
Dietary Fiber 1 g	
Sugars 19 g	
Protein 3 g	
Calcium 44 mg	
Iron 1 mg	

Pumpkin Layered Dessert

CRUST:

½ cup white flour

½ cup oat flour

2 tbsp. sugar or Splenda®

½ cup Smart Balance® regular spread, softened

SECOND LAYER

8 oz. light cream cheese, softened

1 cup powdered sugar

1 (12-oz.) tub frozen whipped topping, thawed

THIRD LAYER:

1 (16-oz.) can pumpkin puree

2 (1.5-oz.) pkg. sugar-free instant vanilla pudding mix

1 cup half and half

1 tsp. cinnamon

½ tsp. ginger

¼ tsp. ground cloves

TOPPING:

Chopped walnuts

Combine crust ingredients. Press into bottom of a 9x13-in. baking pan. Bake 15 min. at 350 degrees, or until golden. Let cool.

For second layer, beat together cream cheese and sugar well. Stir in half the whipped topping. Spread on crust.

Beat together third layer ingredients. Spread over second layer. Chill at least 1 hour.

Top with remaining whipped topping and a sprinkle of chopped walnuts. Yield: 16 servings.

Nutrition Facts
Amount Per Serving
Calories 221 (46% from Fat, 7% from Protein, 47% from Carb)
Total Fat 11 g
Saturated Fat 6 g
Mono Fat 3 g
Cholesterol 14 mg
Sodium 343 mg
Total Carbohydrate 27 g
Dietary Fiber 2 g
Sugars 12 g
Protein 4 g
Calcium 56 mg
Iron 1 mg

Pumpkin Fluff

1 (16-oz.) can pumpkin puree
½ (1.5-oz.) pkg. sugar-free vanilla pudding
  mix
8 oz. frozen whipped topping, thawed
1 tsp. allspice or pumpkin pie spice
½ cup milk, optional

In medium bowl, mix all ingredients thoroughly. Beat by hand 2 min. Refrigerate at least 2 hours in bowl or individual serving bowls. Yield: 4 servings.

Nutrition Facts	
Amount Per Serving	
Calories 247 (53% from Fat, 4% from Protein, 43% from Carb)	
Total Fat 15 g	
Saturated Fat 13 g	
Mono Fat 1 g	
Cholesterol 2 mg	
Sodium 247 mg	
Total Carbohydrate 27 g	
Dietary Fiber 3 g	
Sugars 18 g	
Protein 3 g	
Calcium 61 mg	
Iron 2 mg	

Chocolate Mousse

6 oz. sugar-free or semi-sweet chocolate
  chips
¾ cup milk, scalded
1 egg
2 tbsp. Splenda® or sugar
1 tsp. amaretto or Irish Cream liqueur

Add all ingredients to blender and blend 1 min. Pour into individual serving dishes. Chill at least 1 hour. Yield: 4 servings.

Nutrition Facts	
Amount Per Serving	
Calories 244 (50% from Fat, 7% from Protein, 43% from Carb)	
Total Fat 15 g	
Saturated Fat 8 g	
Mono Fat 5 g	
Cholesterol 64 mg	
Sodium 34 mg	
Total Carbohydrate 29 g	
Dietary Fiber 3 g	
Sugars 25 g	
Protein 4 g	
Calcium 47 mg	
Iron 2 mg	

Chocolate Mousse II

1 (2.1-oz.) pkg. sugar-free instant chocolate
   pudding mix
1½ cups milk
16 oz. frozen whipped topping, thawed

   With wire whisk, mix together pudding
mix and milk until well combined. Fold in
whipped topping. Can be served in parfait
glasses immediately, but keep refrigerated.
Yield: 8 servings.

Nutrition Facts	
Amount Per Serving	
Calories 217 (62% from Fat, 3% from Protein, 35% from Carb)	
Total Fat 15 g	
Saturated Fat 13 g	
Mono Fat 1 g	
Cholesterol 2 mg	
Sodium 238 mg	
Total Carbohydrate 20 g	
Dietary Fiber 1 g	
Sugars 14 g	
Protein 2 g	
Calcium 39 mg	
Iron 1 mg	

Apricot Mousse

1 cup dried apricots
⅔ cup water
⅓ cup Splenda®
1½ tbsp. orange juice
½ tsp. brandy extract
1½ cups whipping cream

   In small saucepan, combine apricots,
water, and Splenda®. Bring mixture to a boil.
Reduce heat and simmer, uncovered, 12
min. Puree in blender or food processor.
   Stir in orange juice and brandy extract.
Cool.
   Beat cream until stiff. Fold into apricot
mixture. Spoon into 6 individual serving
dishes and chill. Yield: 6 servings.

Nutrition Facts	
Amount Per Serving	
Calories 162 (59% from Fat, 3% from Protein, 38% from Carb)	
Total Fat 11 g	
Saturated Fat 7 g	
Mono Fat 3 g	
Cholesterol 41 mg	
Sodium 14 mg	
Total Carbohydrate 16 g	
Dietary Fiber 2 g	
Sugars 12 g	
Protein 1 g	
Calcium 32 mg	
Iron 1 mg	

Lemon Meringue Cups

CUPS:

3 egg whites

½ tsp. white vinegar

¼ tsp. vanilla extract

⅛ tsp. salt

1 cup sugar

CUSTARD:

⅓ cup cornstarch

⅛ tsp. salt

1 cup Splenda®

1½ cups water

3 egg yolks

1 tbsp. lemon zest

6 tbsp. fresh lemon juice

2 tbsp. butter

TOPPING:

Sweetened Whipped Cream (see index)

Lemon zest

For cups, in mixing bowl with electric mixer, combine egg whites, vinegar, vanilla, and salt. Beat until soft peaks form. Gradually add sugar. Continue beating until stiff peaks form.

Cover a baking sheet with parchment paper. Spoon egg mixture into 8 mounds on parchment paper. Shape into cups with a spoon.

Bake 35 min. at 300 degrees. Turn oven off, and let cups dry at least 1 hour in oven with door closed. Remove cups from parchment paper. Store cooled cups in an airtight container until ready to fill.

For custard, in saucepan, combine cornstarch, salt, and Splenda®. Add water and mix well. Cook and stir over medium heat approximately 2 min. until thick and bubbly.

Beat egg yolks. Add a small amount of hot mixture to temper

yolks. Pour into saucepan. Cook and stir 2 additional min. Remove from heat.

Blend in lemon zest, juice, and butter. Chill.

Just before serving, fill meringue cups with custard. Top each with small dollop of whipped cream. Sprinkle zest on top. Yield: 8 servings.

Nutrition Facts
Amount Per Serving
Calories 198 (26% from Fat, 5% from Protein, 69% from Carb)
Total Fat 6 g
Saturated Fat 3 g
Mono Fat 2 g
Cholesterol 90 mg
Sodium 120 mg
Total Carbohydrate 35 g
Dietary Fiber 0 g
Sugars 26 g
Protein 3 g
Calcium 14 mg
Iron 0 mg

Pavlova

4 egg whites
1 cup sugar
1 tsp. vanilla extract
1 tsp. lemon juice
2 tsp. cornstarch
Sweetened Whipped Cream (see index)
Sliced fruit

Be sure absolutely no grease or egg yolk are allowed into the egg whites, or this recipe will not work properly. In large bowl with electric mixer, beat egg whites until stiff but not dry. Gradually add sugar, 1 tbsp. at a time, beating well after each addition. Continue beating until thick and glossy, but do not overbeat. Gently fold in vanilla, lemon juice, and cornstarch.

Line a baking sheet with parchment paper that has been crumpled, smoothed out, and dusted with cornstarch. Draw a 9-in. circle on the parchment paper. Spoon mixture inside circle. Working from center, spread mixture toward outside edge, building up at edge slightly. There should be a deep indentation in the center.

Bake 1 hour in a preheated 300-degree oven. Turn off oven but leave meringue inside at least 1 hour to dry.

Remove paper and place meringue on flat serving plate. Fill center with whipped cream. Arrange fruit attractively around whipped cream. Yield: 8 servings.

Nutrition Facts	
Amount Per Serving	
Calories 220 (45% from Fat, 5% from Protein, 51% from Carb)	
Total Fat 11 g	
Saturated Fat 7 g	
Mono Fat 3 g	
Cholesterol 41 mg	
Sodium 39 mg	
Total Carbohydrate 28 g	
Dietary Fiber 0 g	
Sugars 26 g	
Protein 3 g	
Calcium 24 mg	
Iron 0 mg	

Chapter 12
Miscellaneous Recipes

For a grand finale, here are miscellaneous recipes that do not conveniently fit into any other category but are worthy of inclusion nonetheless.

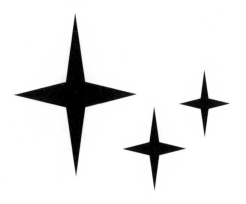

Ambrosia

3 oranges, peeled and sectioned
3 bananas, sliced
¼ cup shredded coconut
Splenda® to taste
Slivered almonds or 4 maraschino cherries

Cut orange sections in thirds and add to small bowl. Add bananas, coconut, and Splenda®. Toss. Chill several hours.

Serve in individual glass serving dishes. Top each serving with almonds or 1 cherry. Can also be layered with sugar-free pudding in parfait glasses. Yield: 4 servings.

Nutrition Facts	
Amount Per Serving	
Calories 177 (3% from Fat, 6% from Protein, 91% from Carb)	
Total Fat 1 g	
Saturated Fat 0 g	
Mono Fat 0 g	
Cholesterol 0 mg	
Sodium 2 mg	
Total Carbohydrate 44 g	
Dietary Fiber 6 g	
Sugars 27 g	
Protein 3 g	
Calcium 68 mg	
Iron 1 mg	

French Pears

8 large, ripe pears, peeled
1 (8-oz.) pkg. cream cheese
½-1 cup chopped pecans
2 tbsp. Splenda® or powdered sugar
Chocolate Sauce (see below), warm
Chopped pecans for garnish, optional

Slice each pear lengthwise and remove core, taking care to keep pear halves intact. Mix cream cheese, pecans, and Splenda® or sugar. Carefully stuff mixture into cavity of each pear half. Put each pear half together to form whole pears again; wrap individually with plastic wrap.

Store in covered container until chilled and ready to serve, preferably within 12 hours. To serve, place 1 pear in stemmed sherbet glass, pour sauce over top, and sprinkle with additional pecans, if desired. Yield: 8 servings.

Nutrition Facts

Amount Per Serving

Calories 235 (36% from Fat, 7% from Protein, 57% from Carb)

Total Fat 10 g	
Saturated Fat 4 g	
Mono Fat 4 g	
Cholesterol 16 mg	
Sodium 86 mg	
Total Carbohydrate 36 g	
Dietary Fiber 7 g	
Sugars 21 g	
Protein 4 g	
Calcium 55 mg	
Iron 1 mg	

Chocolate Sauce

1 cup cocoa powder
2 cups Splenda®
1¼ cups hot water
Dash salt
2 tsp. vanilla extract

In saucepan, combine first 4 ingredients. Boil 3 min. Add vanilla.

Serve hot. Store excess in refrigerator. This is great on ice cream. Yield: 10 servings.

Nutrition Facts

Amount Per Serving

Calories 41 (18% from Fat, 11% from Protein, 70% from Carb)

Total Fat 1 g	
Saturated Fat 1 g	
Mono Fat 0 g	
Cholesterol 0 mg	
Sodium 2 mg	
Total Carbohydrate 10 g	
Dietary Fiber 3 g	
Sugars 0 g	
Protein 2 g	
Calcium 10 mg	
Iron 1 mg	

Chocolate Gravy

¾ cup Splenda®
3 tbsp. cocoa powder
3 tbsp. flour
Pinch salt
1½ cups milk
½ tsp. vanilla extract

In small saucepan, mix together dry ingredients. Add milk. Cook over low heat, stirring constantly, until thickened, approximately 10 min. Should be the consistency of pudding.

Stir in vanilla. Serve warm over split biscuits for breakfast. Yield: 6 servings.

Note: You may add 1 tbsp. butter before serving.

Nutrition Facts

Amount Per Serving

Calories 70 (29% from Fat, 16% from Protein, 55% from Carb)

Total Fat 2 g	
Saturated Fat 1 g	
Mono Fat 1 g	
Cholesterol 6 mg	
Sodium 25 mg	
Total Carbohydrate 10 g	
Dietary Fiber 1 g	
Sugars 3 g	
Protein 3 g	
Calcium 73 mg	
Iron 1 mg	

Ice Cream Sandwiches

No-sugar-added fat-free ice cream, softened
2 graham crackers or homemade reduced-sugar cookies

Spread ice cream between bottoms of graham crackers or cookies. Wrap and freeze several hours. Yield: 1 serving.

Nutrition Facts		
Amount Per Serving		
Calories 186 (27% from Fat, 8% from Protein, 64% from Carb)		
Total Fat 6 g		
Saturated Fat 2 g		
Mono Fat 2 g		
Cholesterol 7 mg		
Sodium 210 mg		
Total Carbohydrate 30 g		
Dietary Fiber 1 g		
Sugars 13 g		
Protein 4 g		
Calcium 92 mg		
Iron 1 mg		

Net Carb Counter

Net carbs mean that fiber has been subtracted. Net carbs listed here are approximate and may vary by brand.

Chocolate and Cocoa

chocolate, bittersweet or semi-sweet	1 oz. = 8g
chocolate, sugar-free or unsweetened	1 oz. = 3.84g
chocolate chips, semi-sweet	1 tbsp. = 9g
chocolate chips, unsweetened	1 tbsp. = 8g
chocolate syrup, sugar-free such as Smucker's®	2 tbsp. = 22g
cocoa, unsweetened	1 tbsp. = 3g

Dairy and Substitutes

cheese, cheddar, regular	1 oz. = 0g
cottage cheese, low-fat 1% milk fat	½ cup = 3g
cream cheese, regular	2 tbsp. = 1g
cream cheese, light	2 oz. = 2g
egg, whole, large	1 = 0.39g
egg, white, large	1 = 0.24g
egg, yolk, large	1 = 0.61g
cream, heavy	1 tbsp. = 0.83g
cream, heavy	½ cup = 3.32g
half-and-half	2 tbsp. = 1g
whipped topping, frozen non-dairy	2 tbsp. = 2g
buttermilk, whole	1 cup = 8g
milk, whole	1 cup = 13g
milk, skim	1 cup = 11.98g
milk, 1%	1 cup = 12g
milk, 2%	1 cup = 13g
milk, soy	1 cup = 8g
milk, sweetened condensed, regular	2 tbsp. = 21g
milk, evaporated, whole	2 tbsp. = 3g
yogurt, plain, whole-milk	1 cup = 11g

yogurt, plain, low-fat   1 cup = 16g
yogurt, plain, fat-free   1 cup = 18g

Fats and Oils

butter   0g
canola butter   0g
canola oil   0g
olive oil   0g
shortening, trans-fat-free   0g
Smart Balance® regular spread   0g

Flours

all-purpose flour   1 cup = 92.01g
almond flour   1 cup = 12g
amaranth flour   1 cup = 99.39g
barley flour   1 cup = 95.34g
bean flour, white   1 cup = 48g
bread flour   1 cup = 84g
buckwheat flour   1 cup = 72.71g
cake flour   1 cup = 92g
coconut flour   1 cup = 5g
flaxseed flour   1 cup = 0g
graham flour   1 cup = 80g
oat flour   1 cup = 48g
quinoa flour   1 cup = 68g
rice flour, brown   1 cup = 113.57g
rice flour, white   1 cup = 122.81g
rye flour, medium   1 cup = 64.15g
soy flour   1 cup = 24g
spelt flour   1 cup = 76g
white whole-wheat flour   1 cup = 72g
whole-wheat flour   1 cup = 72g
whole-wheat pastry flour   1 cup = 76g

Fruit, Fruit Juices, and Vegetables

apple, 1 small (4 oz.)	17g
applesauce, unsweetened	½ cup = 12g
apricots, canned halves in heavy syrup, drained	1 cup = 40.76g
banana, 1 small ripe	3½ oz. = 20g
blackberries	1 cup = 6.21g
blueberries	¾ cup = 13g
coconut, sweetened, flaked	2 tbsp. = 5g
cranberries	½ cup = 4g
dates, pitted	1 oz. = 19g
fruit preserves, sugar-free	1 tbsp. = 5g
mango, 1 small	3½ oz. = 15g
maraschino cherry	1 cherry = 2g
peach, 1 med.	4 oz. = 9g
peaches, canned slices in light syrup	½ cup = 16g
pineapple, canned crushed	½ cup = 14g
pineapple, canned slices in heavy syrup	2 slices = 22g
raisins	¼ cup = 31g
raspberries	1 cup = 7g
strawberries, whole fresh	1 cup = 8g
strawberries, frozen, unsweetened	1 cup = 13.60g
strawberries, frozen, sweetened, sliced	1 cup = 63.85g
lemon juice	1 tsp. = 0g
orange juice	½ cup = 13g
carrots	½ cup = 4g
pumpkin, canned, pure	½ cup = 4g
sweet potato, large, cooked	31.34g
zucchini	½ cup = 2g

Nuts, Seeds, and Spreads

almonds, sliced	1 cup = 7.30g
almonds, slivered	1 cup = 8.58g
almonds, whole	1 cup = 11.36g
flaxseed	1 tbsp. = 0g
hazelnuts, chopped	1 cup = 8.05g
peanuts, oil-roasted with salt, chopped	1 cup = 8.43g
pecans, chopped	1 cup = 4.65
walnuts, chopped	1 cup = 8.20g
Nutella®	2 tbsp. = 22g
peanut butter	1 cup = 32.30g

Rice and Grains

cornmeal, white or yellow	1 cup = 84.90g
oat bran	1 cup = 47.7g
rice, brown, cooked	½ cup = 20g
rice, white, cooked, long-grain	½ cup = 22g
rolled oats, old-fashioned, dry	½ cup = 23g
tapioca, dry, pearl	1 cup = 133.44g
wheat bran, dry	1 cup = 12.60g
wheat germ	1 cup = 44.39g

Sugar and Substitutes

corn syrup	1 tsp. = 5g
honey	1 tsp. = 6g
molasses, blackstrap	1 tbsp. = 15g
NutraSweet®	2 tbsp. = 21g
sugar, white granular	1 tsp. = 4g
sugar, brown	1 tsp. = 4g
Splenda®	1 tsp. = 1g
Splenda® Brown Sugar Blend	1 tsp. = 1g

Miscellaneous

frosting, reduced-sugar, tub chocolate	2 tbsp. = 15g
graham cracker crumbs	3 tbsp. = 13g
Jell-O®, sugar-free	0.3 oz. pkg. = 0g
pudding, sugar-free vanilla made with fat-free milk	½ cup = 6g

Index